Canadian
Outdoor
Cookbook
Camping • BBQ • Picnics

Jeff Morrison
and James Darcy

www.companyscoming.com
visit our website

Canadian Outdoor Cookbook

First Printing November 2012

Library and Archives Canada Cataloguing in Publication
Morrison, Jeff, 1967–
    Canadian outdoor cookbook / Jeff Morrison & James Darcy.
(Wild Canada series)
Includes index.
ISBN 978-1-897477-68-7
    1. Outdoor cooking. 2. Cookbooks. I. Darcy, James II. Title.
III. Series: Wild Canada series
TX823.M674 2013   641.5'78   C2012-906883-7

Published by
Company's Coming Publishing Limited
2311–96 Street NW
Edmonton, Alberta, Canada T6N 1G3
Tel: 780-450-6223 Fax: 780-450-1857
www.companyscoming.com

Cover image: © FOODCOLLECTION / Stock Food Canada (for grilled food on barbecue);
        © Thinkstock / Comstock / Getty Images (for background area behind the barbecue)

We gratefully acknowledge the following suppliers for their generous support of our Test and Photography Kitchens: Barbecue Country (p. 51); Campers' Village (p. 70, p. 124).

Company's Coming is a registered trademark owned by Company's Coming Publishing Limited.

We acknowledge the financial support of the Government of Canada through the Canada Book Fund for our publishing activities.

Printed in China

PC: 21

Table of Contents

Snacks And Sandwiches
Appetizers
Snacks
Soup
Sandwiches

Mains Dishes
Beef and Game
Lamb and Pork
Poultry
Fish and Seafood

Sides and Salads

Sauces

Breakfasts

Sweets and Drinks

Introduction

Spending time in the great outdoors beneath the stars is as typically Canadian as s'mores and thick-sliced bacon. Camping, tenting and cottaging—pastimes enjoyed by hoards of people in this country—are becoming more popular among urbanites than ever before. Spending time outdoors has what can best be described as a healing effect on the soul. Just ask anyone who frequents the Canadian wilderness and they will likely recount the many rejuvenating properties of long hours spent afield.

According to Statistics Canada, in the third quarter of 2005 alone, Canadians spent a whopping 17.3 million nights at campgrounds. By comparison, only 14.8 million nights were spent in hotels and motels during the same time period. Yes, it is true, we do enjoy getting back to nature, and it shows. Outdoor enthusiasts live for the brief moments in which they can trade the hustle and bustle of the city for the sight of a meteor shower at night or the echo of a coyote's howl over the ridge.

When getting away from town to experience what Mother Nature has to offer, we have varying preferences. Some like to rough it in a tent or even construct their own primitive lean-to or shelter, while others prefer the warmth of a chalet, cottage or camp. The one aspect that none of us hope to scrimp on when outdoors is the food we eat. As our interest in spending time camping and sleeping in the outdoors increases, so too does our ability to whip up a well-thought-out meal, cooked on the open fire or barbecue in a wonderful outdoor setting. There is a certain sense of accomplishment in putting together a good meal without the modern convenience of electricity.

At every step in your journey to cook outdoors, this handy cookbook will be there to assist. The recipes I have selected for this book run the gamut of culinary styles and flavours. These meals cover a virtual cornucopia of tastes—which, as I have discovered, come to life when cooking in the fresh northern air. These dishes represent what I believe cooking outdoors is meant to be. I have picked up a few tricks over the past 40 years that I have spent enjoying the nature lifestyle, and I will share those with you along the way. For those who enjoy camping, fishing, hunting or eco-tourism, the *Canadian Outdoor Cookbook* may one day rank up there with the beloved dragonfly (that snaps up mosquitoes!) as the camper's best friend.

About Outdoor Cooking

Hand Test

There are a few specialized and essential cooking techniques that will undoubtedly make your outdoor cooking experience a more pleasant one. Establishing the approximate temperature of a campfire, for example, is one of the most important skills you can learn when preparing meals in the great outdoors. Determining the precise temperature of a campfire is nearly impossible without the use of a sophisticated thermometer, but there is a simple heat test that uses only your hands, which many people find, well, handy.

For this test, you need to hold your hand about 3 to 4 inches (7.5 to 10 centimetres) off the grill. If you're able to hold it there for only 1 to 2 seconds before pulling it away, the temperature is considered high. Heat of this magnitude is used mostly for searing beef and is usually too hot for other uses. If you're able to hold your hand there for 2 to 3 seconds before pulling it away, the temperature is considered medium, and is suitable for a variety of pork and fish dishes. About 4 to 5 seconds would mean medium-low and is great for vegetables. About 7 to 8 seconds would be considered low and the temperature is suitable for, say, warming hot dog or hamburger buns.

Heat Sources

There are more types of heat sources for outdoor cooking than you can shake a stick at, and one is no better than the next. It is all a matter of taste and convenience. One camper may opt for an easy gas barbecue; however, they do tend to be cumbersome. Another may choose an old-school Hibachi as the grill of choice, and that's just fine. Still others want to go traditional with an all-wood cooking fire. Although it depends greatly on the wood used, a general rule of thumb is that most cooking fires take at least 1 hour to produce coals suitable for cooking on. A wood or propane oven is an appliance usually found in most camps and cottages, and is required for a small number of recipes in this book.

The most important thing to remember when cooking outdoors is that you are away from a conventional kitchen. The cooking and meal choices you make while spending time in the wilderness, regardless of what they are, should be relaxed and easygoing to match your surroundings. First and foremost, spending time away from home is meant to be fun and stress-free!

Outdoor Cooking Tools

There are a few small items and cooking utensils one should always have when travelling into the backwoods this summer. Here are just a few essential items every outdoor chef should have on hand at all times: aluminum foil, non-stick cooking spray, skewers (metal and wood), oven mitts or pot holders, fire igniter, extra cooking oil, paper towels, a paring knife, a fillet knife, a meat saw, scissors, an axe, a shovel and a camping cooler.

Cooking Tips and Terminology

Whether you are cooking with a gas barbecue, a Coleman-style camping stove, over the campfire coals or on a propane stove, there are a few things you need to know. A Coleman-style stove can be a great asset in the outdoors, provided you know how to set one up. Most camping stoves run on naphtha fuel, but some use propane. Be sure to use only the fuel specified on your stove. Never refill a camp stove with fuel inside the tent or cottage, because fuel is extremely flammable. A campfire suitable for cooking is one that has burned down to a nice bed of hot coals. When cooking over a campfire, we generally use what is referred to as a cooking "grid" or "grate," which is basically a portable cooking grill similar to the cooking surface of a gas barbecue. Positioning your campfire grid over the coals is also very important. A small handful of baseball-sized rocks positioned around the coals make a great support for your cooking grid. A good height from the coals is typically 2–3 inches (5–7.5 centimetres), unless the recipe calls for more or less clearance.

Plank Cooking

Plank cooking is an interesting twist on regular grilling and there are a couple of things you will need to know before getting started.

6

Regardless of where you get your plank or what type of wood it is, every plank must be prepared in advance and soaked before it can be used for cooking. Soak the plank in a pail or bucket of water for at least 1 hour. Some people even like to add a few ingredients to the water, such as salt or wine. I often add a cup or two of apple juice—it gives the wood a nice aroma when cooking. Another important step before cooking with your plank the first time is the "toasting stage." Once the plank has soaked for at least 1 hour, place it on a medium grill and toast for 5 minutes on each side. This will bring out a smokier flavour in whatever meat you cook on the plank. Plank cooking is a great way to give a smoked flavour to your food without having to use a conventional smoker.

Rotisserie

A rotisserie is a system whereby meat is suspended and rotated above a heat source such as a gas barbecue or campfire grill. Most rotisseries are electric but some are also manual crank-style. Rotisseries are a fabulous way to cook whole chickens because they offer very even heat distribution. Depending on your resourcefulness, if you have any welding experience for example, you could even make your own rotisserie from steel reinforcement bars. The most important components of a rotisserie are a stable attachment device for the meat, often a set of skewers or a metal cage, and a solid stand so that the meat remains a set distance away from the heat source.

A Few Helpful Tips

Hot Campfire Chicken Wings

(see photo p. 33)

Serves 6 to 8

Chicken wings are a popular white meat in Canada for young and old alike, and they can be served in a variety of different ways. But did you know that the wings of waterfowl (ducks, geese and most game bird species) are actually considered a dark meat? The reason is simple. Chickens do not fly and therefore rarely use their wings for any practical purpose, causing the meat to be white in colour. Wild game birds, on the other hand, spend much of their time flying, which explains why their wings are dark meat. The more a bird uses a certain body part, the darker the meat becomes. The same explanation applies to why chicken legs are dark meat whereas many wild birds have lighter meat on their legs.

> 4 lbs (1.8 kg) pre-cut chicken wings
> 2 Tbsp (30 mL) olive oil
> salt, to taste
>
> 1/4 cup (60 mL) butter, melted
> 1/4 cup (60 mL) hot sauce
> 1 1/2 Tbsp (25 mL) cider vinegar

Prepare campfire, or preheat grill to medium. Place chicken wings in large bowl and add olive oil and a few pinches of salt. Mix well to coat wings. Place wings on grill and cook for about 30 minutes.

Meanwhile, combine butter, hot sauce and vinegar and add salt to taste. Mix well. Once wings are thoroughly cooked, add to sauce and toss to coat evenly. Serve with your favourite blue-cheese dipping sauce and celery and/or carrot sticks.

Cheese Fondue in the Great Outdoors

Serves 4

I find that a good cheese fondue is best enjoyed later on in the evening after the little ones have been bundled up in their sleeping bags. The adults can sit around the fire enjoying this traditional European recipe. Cheese fondues have been a huge part of Swiss tradition for generations. Back in the 1930s, Switzerland's Swiss Cheese Union deemed the cheese fondue a national dish. It was a way to increase the country's consumption of cheese products, and evidently it worked. The cheese fondue soon also became a tradition of many other parts of the world.

1 cup (250 mL) shredded Cheddar cheese
1 cup (250 mL) shredded Swiss cheese
2 Tbsp (30 mL) flour
1 × 10 oz (284 mL) can condensed cream of chicken soup
1/2 × 12 1/2 oz (355 mL) can beer

1 loaf French bread, cubed

Prepare campfire, or preheat grill to low. In pot, combine cheeses, flour, soup and beer. Mix well and stir over heat until cheese has melted. Transfer to fondue pot and enjoy with bread cubes.

Homemade Hummus

Serves 4

The only thing better than snacking on hummus is making your own. And there is no better time to make your own hummus than during a wonderful outdoor excursion. Did you know that in addition to being a tasty treat, hummus is also very nutritious? It is high in fibre and low in fat, and boasts high levels of iron, magnesium, zinc and vitamin B, among other things. Hummus is actually one of the oldest snack foods known to man, dating back over 7000 years to the ancient Egyptians.

2 × 12 oz (341 mL) cans chickpeas, drained
2 Tbsp (30 mL) olive oil
6 Tbsp (90 mL) tahini (sesame paste)
juice of 3 lemons
water, as needed
4 garlic cloves, minced

Using fork or potato masher, thoroughly mash chickpeas in bowl. Add olive oil, tahini and lemon juice. If mixture is too thick, add water as needed. Stir in garlic. Serve with pita bread or crackers.

Grilled Marinated Mushrooms

Serves 4 to 6 as an appetizer

One task that is often overlooked by campers is finding suitable fuel and firewood for your cooking fire or campfire. There are three main ingredients for good campfire: the first is the igniters, or a catalyst such as flint fire starter or paper; the second is dry kindling such as pine or cedar; and the last ingredient is the main dry firewood, typically hardwood such as birch, maple or oak. Finding these around your campsite may be difficult if you have not done your homework. It is suggested that firewood is dried for at least one year to create a good cooking fire. Some camping areas sell what is called kiln-dried wood, which is basically a speedier (yet more expensive) process for extracting moisture from green firewood.

1 1/2 cups (375 mL) butter
1/2 cup (125 mL) soy (or teriyaki) sauce
3 Tbsp (45 mL) olive oil
2 Tbsp (30 mL) balsamic vinegar
1 tsp (5 mL) sugar
3/4 tsp (4 mL) garlic powder
3/4 tsp (4 mL) ginger
1/2 tsp (2 mL) pepper

1 lb (454 g) white mushrooms

In saucepan, melt butter and add remaining ingredients except mushrooms. Mix well and heat. Place mushrooms in bowl and pour marinade over top; stir to coat. Marinate in cooler or refrigerator for 1 to 2 hours.

Prepare campfire, or preheat grill to medium. Remove mushrooms from marinade, reserving marinade. Cook for 5 to 10 minutes, basting occasionally, until mushrooms have softened. Remove from grill and serve.

Old-fashioned Campfire Bannock

Serves 4 to 6

Bannock was originally brought to North America by Scottish fur traders. It was quickly adopted by First Nations communities in Canada and the United States. The Métis and Plains First Nations used bannock extensively in their diets, and it still plays a huge role in native culture. Because of how easy it was to prepare and cook in the wilderness, bannock was often served as a bread substitute for breakfast, or as a meal served with meat and fruit. It is a good source of carbohydrates and most people really enjoy the taste. As you sit around the fire enjoying your own homemade bannock, you may want to ponder its cultural importance this summer. Bannock may be eaten on its own, mixed with sweets as a snack, or with meat, fruits and vegetables as a meal.

2 to 3 cups (500 to 750 mL) flour
1 to 2 Tbsp (15 to 30 mL) baking powder
2 to 3 Tbsp (30 to 45 mL) oil, butter or lard
1 tsp (5 mL) salt
2/3 cup (150 mL) warm water

Prepare campfire. Place flour, baking powder, oil and salt in bowl and mix with your hands until dough clumps. Slowly add water and mix until dough softens. Wrap handful of dough around end of freshly cut, very green branch. Massage dough so it remains together. Cook over coals for about 10 minutes, rotating to cook evenly.

Classic Beanie Weenies

Serves 6 to 8

When I was a boy in the early 1970s, Beanie Weenies was an outdoor mainstay of children my age. Not only did it taste great every time, eating it automatically gave us the right to sing the "beans, beans, the magical fruit" song. It was one of those meals you never forget. It was always fun to have Beanie Weenies for dinner...and the after-effects of this old-fashioned family favourite were also of some strange amusement for most kids I knew! It does not seem to matter what dish you add wieners to—for some reason it always makes it taste better.

1 × 14 oz (398 mL) can baked beans
1 package all-beef wieners
1/2 medium onion, diced
1 Tbsp (15 mL) prepared mustard
1 Tbsp (15 mL) ketchup
1 Tbsp (15 mL) brown sugar

Prepare campfire, or preheat grill to medium. Pour beans into large skillet or cast-iron frying pan. Slice wieners into small pieces and add to beans. Add onion, mustard, ketchup and brown sugar and mix. Simmer for 20 to 30 minutes.

Homemade Potato Chips

Serves 4

Some recipes, such as this one, require the use of an oven—gas, wood or electric. Since camp and cottage ovens tend to fluctuate more in temperature than ovens in homes, I often use a cooking thermometer as a gauge. The old wood-stove oven at my camp does have a temperature dial on the door, but it is rather inaccurate—a portable thermometer is much more reliable. Keep in mind that regulating the temperature of a wood-stove oven will take some practice. A trick I have learned is to prop the door open slightly if the temperature rises too high. However, using a propane or electric oven is not quite so labour-intensive.

> 4 baking potatoes, washed, peeled and
>   sliced diagonally, 1/8 inch (3 mm) thick
> 1/4 cup (60 mL) melted butter
> salt

Preheat camp or cottage oven to 450°F (230°C). Arrange potato slices on greased baking sheet without overlapping. Brush slices with butter and bake for 15 to 20 minutes until golden brown and crispy. Sprinkle with salt and enjoy.

Sweet Potato Fries

(*see* photo p. 70)

Serves 6

The first time I was introduced to Sweet Potato Fries was during the Ottawa Bluesfest, a popular annual music festival in downtown Ottawa each July. One of the local restaurants was on-site serving their own "secret French-fry recipe," and concert-goers were simply going crazy for them! I could tell right away that these golden bits of heaven were made with sweet potatoes instead of regular potatoes. For some reason, the natural sweetness of the sweet potato simply bursts to life when prepared in strings and deep-fried in oil.

> 4 sweet potatoes
> 1 tsp (5 mL) salt
> 1/4 tsp (1 mL) pepper
> 1/2 tsp (2 mL) paprika
> 1/4 tsp (1 mL) garlic powder
>
> 3 Tbsp (45 mL) olive oil
> 1/2 tsp (2 mL) parsley

Preheat oven to 400°F (205°C). Peel and cut sweet potatoes into 1/2-inch (12 mm) slices; place in large bowl. In small bowl, combine salt, pepper, paprika and garlic powder.

Pour olive oil over potato slices. Add parsley and mix well. Sprinkle in seasoning mixture and toss to coat. Place seasoned fries on greased baking sheet in single layer. Cook for about 45 minutes, turning once.

Tube Steaks with Bacon and Cheese

Serves 4 to 6

I will never forget a camping trip to Alma, New Brunswick, on the shores of the magnificent Bay of Fundy, where the highest tides in the world roll in and out. While my wife Cheryl and I sat by the campfire one night, we watched as a group of six raccoons systematically made their way up the hill and into the campground. We chuckled as we watched other campers scramble to conceal their coolers and stow away their food supplies. After years of camping, you learn how to be prepared for scavengers, not leaving a single food scrap around. You could just tell these raccoons had snuck food from campers before. I will never forget how comical it was to see one raccoon as he scurried away from a neighbouring tent with a hot dog in his mouth. It looked like he was smoking a big cigar!

> 6 hot dogs
> thin slices Cheddar cheese, cut into 1/2-inch (12 mm) pieces
> 6 strips bacon
> 6 hot dog buns

Prepare campfire, or preheat grill to medium. Slice wieners lengthwise without cutting right through. Fill with Cheddar cheese slices. Wrap piece of bacon around each hot dog, covering it completely.

Place hot dogs on grill, cheese-side down, and cook, covered, for 2 minutes. Turn and keep cooking for 3 to 4 minutes until bacon is cooked through and crisp. Place hot dogs in buns, and top with your favourite condiments.

Honey Soy Sausages

Serves 4 to 6

This recipe is great not only because of its taste but also because of its versatility. Sure, it makes a fabulous dinner, but why stop there? We have enjoyed cooking this dish later in the evening when our fellow campers were looking for a snack. There's nothing like perfectly cooked Honey Soy Sausages on the open grill. Perhaps it's the natural wood flavouring or simply the fact that you're enjoying them in the greatest backdrop on Earth. Camping is something every Canadian should do at least once in their lifetime. The problem is that once you're bitten by the camping bug, you will want to do it all the time!

> 1/3 cup (75 mL) honey
> 1/3 cup (75 mL) soy sauce
> 1 garlic clove, crushed
> 1 × 1 1/4-inch (3 cm) piece fresh ginger,
>   peeled and finely grated
> 1 Tbsp (15 mL) sweet sherry
> 1 sprig fresh thyme
>
> 8 to 10 thick pork or beef sausages

Combine all ingredients except sausages in bowl and mix well. Add sausages and turn to coat. Cover and place in cooler or refrigerator for 6 to 8 hours.

Prepare campfire, or preheat grill to medium. Grease grill with non-stick cooking spray. Remove sausages from marinade, reserving marinade. Cook sausages for 5 to 6 minutes, turning frequently and brushing occasionally with marinade.

Bean and Bacon Soup

Serves 10

With the advent of modern technology came the introduction of the popular two-way radio, or "walkie-talkie" as some still call them. My feeling has always been that since the technology is there, why not take advantage of it? I have several sets of two-way radios I use during my trips into the great outdoors. General Mobile Radio Service (GMRS) radios have a longer range than the Family Radio Service (FRS) on the market. Radios are a must for anyone with younger children who plan to be off on their own. I have a small set of FRS two-way radios that have an effective range of about two miles and are easy for my children to operate. Every time they leave the trailer to walk the dog, visit friends or search for frogs in the nearby creek, we make sure they carry a two-way radio for safety. These items are reasonably priced and add a level of safety when spending time away from home.

2 1/2 cups (625 mL) dried navy beans
12 cups (3 L) water

8 slices bacon
3 onions, chopped

2 cups (500 mL) diced, peeled potato
1 cup (250 mL) sliced carrot
1 × 48 oz (1.36 L) can tomato juice
1 tsp (5 mL) salt
1 tsp (5 mL) pepper

Prepare campfire, or preheat grill to medium. In large pot or Dutch oven, combine beans and water and boil for 20 minutes. Remove from heat, cover and let stand for 1 hour.

In separate pan, cook bacon until crisp. Transfer to paper towels to drain and then crumble. Set aside. Cook onions in oil or bacon drippings until translucent.

Add onions to pot with beans and cook over low for 1 hour. Add bacon, potato, carrot, tomato juice, salt and pepper and cook for 1 hour, stirring occasionally.

Beef Tenderloin Sandwich

Serves 6

Steve Enright of Orleans, Ontario, has camped in *La Belle Province* every spring for the past 22 years and has picked up a few tricks along the way. On a trip north of Sainte-Anne-du-Lac in 1993, he learned the merits of sheltering a campfire on windy days when cooking steaks on the grill. After getting his campfire down to a suitable layer of coals for properly searing his beef tenderloin, Steve positioned his outdoor cooking grid over top and started cooking. Within minutes, a gust of wind blew across the bed of coals, sending sand and debris all over his precious meal. Since Steve had not created a shelter or windbreak around the fire, there was nothing to stop debris from blowing in. From then on, Steve's campfires have been built with removable sheets of tin as a wind shelter just in case, because no one wants ruined tenderloin twice!

1 cup (250 mL) sour cream
2 Tbsp (30 mL) prepared horseradish
1 tsp (5 mL) Dijon mustard

1 × 2 to 2 1/2 lb (900 g to 1.2 kg) centre-cut beef tenderloin
3 Tbsp (45 mL) olive oil
1/2 tsp (2 mL) salt
1/2 tsp (2 mL) pepper

1 to 2 large French baguettes, sliced in half lengthwise
6 leaves iceberg lettuce
1 cup (250 mL) grated Parmesan cheese

Prepare campfire, or preheat grill to high. In small bowl, combine sour cream, horseradish and mustard. Mix well and set aside.

Brush tenderloin with olive oil and sprinkle with salt and pepper. Grill for about 8 minutes to sear meat, then reduce heat to medium and cook for about 20 minutes until tenderloin is firm and pink in centre. Remove from grill and cut into very thin (1/8 inch [3 mm]) slices.

Brush one side of baguette with olive oil and grill on medium to low for about 30 seconds until just lightly toasted. Remove from grill. Spread sour cream mixture on bread and layer with lettuce and tenderloin slices. Top with Parmesan cheese and serve.

Pie Iron Croque-monsieur

Serves 4

The *croque-monsieur* is a traditional French ham and cheese sandwich composed of sourdough bread, Cheddar cheese and any of several types of ham. The beauty of a croque-monsieur cooked over the open fire is the deliciously smoky flavour of the melted cheese and heated ham. They are simply melt-in-your-mouth good! Although there are several ways to make a croque-monsieur, the simplest way when you're outdoors is with a tool known as a "pie iron" or grilled-cheese maker. It features long metal rods and wooden handles to keep your hands cool. Several companies manufacture pie irons for camping, and my favourite brand is the Cuisor. The croque-monsieur maker is something you may want to invest in if you plan to do a lot of outdoor cooking this year.

> **8 slices sourdough bread**
> **2 Tbsp (30 mL) butter**
> **4 slices Cheddar cheese**
> **8 slices Black Forest ham**

Prepare campfire. Butter 1 side of 2 slices of bread. Place 1 slice of bread (butter-side down) on 1 side of pie iron. Add 1 slice of cheese and 2 slices of ham, and top with second slice of bread (butter-side up). Close iron and trim any excess bread so it does not catch fire. Heat over hot coals until cheese has melted and bread is lightly toasted. Repeat for 3 remaining sandwiches.

Forked-stick Ham and Cheese

(*see* photo p. 34)

Serves 2

For Brian Houle of Stittsville, Ontario, and his dad, the traditional *croque-monsieur* (ham and cheese) sandwich is put together with a rustic twist. Brian's father would take him hunting in the Birch Run forest near Cranberry Lake north of Blind River, and after a long morning in the woods they always sat down for their favourite Forked-stick Ham and Cheese for lunch. Brian recalls how they searched for the perfect spot in the bush to build a fire, and then looked for a couple of two-pronged sticks perfect for grilling. It was a great bonding experience for the two, sitting there whittling their cooking utensils. His dad explained how green sapling worked best because it never caught on fire. The classic Forked-stick Ham and Cheese is a tradition Brian has since passed along to his own sons. What would we Canadians be without great outdoor traditions like this to pass down through the generations?

> 4 slices white bread
> 2 Tbsp (30 mL) butter
> 4 slices Cheddar cheese
> 4 thick slices smoked ham

Prepare campfire. Butter 1 side of 2 slices of bread. Place 1 slice of bread (butter-side down) on two-pronged stick whittled from green sapling. Add 1 slice of Cheddar cheese and 1 slice of ham. Place over hot coals and toast slowly. When cheese has melted and bread is lightly toasted, add second slice of bread (butter-side up) and turn over to toast. Repeat for second sandwich and enjoy.

Lunch on a Stick

Make as many as you need

This is an outdoor recipe that's about as simple as any I can think of. In fact, you don't even need a heat source because there is no cooking required. For those days when the fish are really biting and you don't even have time to pull your lines in, you will appreciate Lunch on a Stick. Sure, a full-fledged shore lunch is nice when you have the time, but if you don't feel like making a big fuss at lunch time, you can prepare this meal for the group first thing in the morning and then store it in plastic containers. The great thing about it is you can add whatever you like to each skewer depending on your taste.

> lunch meat of your choice
>   (have your butcher cut it about 1/4 inch [6 mm] thick)
> Cheddar or marble cheese, cut into 1/2-inch (12 mm) cubes
> lettuce, cut into 1/2-inch (12 mm) shreds
> cherry or grape tomatoes
> olives, gherkins or baby dill pickles

Thread lunch meat, cheese cubes, lettuce, tomatoes and olives or pickles onto wooden or metal skewers, alternating as you like. You can use other ingredients as you wish (mushrooms, pieces of onion, bread cubes, bell pepper slices, etc.). Serve and enjoy.

Pie Iron Pizza

(*see* photo p. 51)

Serves 1

Hey, just because your pie iron has been washed and put away after last night's dinner doesn't mean you can't use it again. The great thing about pie irons is that they can cook several different foods over the heat of your campfire. Pizza is a great meal you can create with your pie irons—and the whole family can get involved. The key to cooking any food in a pie iron is to keep it away from direct flame and allow the coals to fully heat the metal surface of the pie iron. You may need to open the pie iron occasionally to check on it, but after you cook a few different foods this way, you will begin to get a feel for how close to the heat to position them, and for how long you need to cook them.

> 2 slices bread
> 2 Tbsp (30 mL) pizza sauce
> 1 slice mozzarella cheese
> pepperoni slices (or green peppers, mushrooms or bacon pieces)

Prepare campfire. Butter 1 side of bread slices. Place 1 slice of bread (butter-side down) on 1 side of pie iron. Spread pizza sauce, cheese slice and pepperoni on bread. Top with second slice of bread (butter-side up). Close iron and trim any excess bread so it does not catch fire. Heat over hot coals until cheese has melted and bread is lightly toasted.

Campfire Pizza

Make as many as you need

If you are spending time in the great outdoors with the kids, Campfire Pizza is the way to go. Be sure to pack enough tortilla shells, though—they tend to disappear quickly. I suggest bringing along 2 packages of tortillas, 2 cans of spaghetti sauce, a 1 lb (454 g) bag of shredded mozzarella cheese and plenty of sliced mushrooms and pepperoni. The only sad part about Campfire Pizza is when it's all gone!

large flour tortillas
spaghetti sauce, homemade or canned
shredded mozzarella cheese
pizza toppings (e.g., sliced pepperoni,
  mushrooms and green peppers)

Prepare campfire. Lay tortilla shell in lightly greased skillet and turn up sides slightly to form raised edge. Spread layer of spaghetti sauce onto tortilla. Sprinkle with cheese and place pizza toppings over top. Cover skillet and hold over hot coals until cheese begins to melt but before tortilla bottom becomes too crispy.

French-style Pizza

Serves 8

A great thing about cooking outdoors is getting the whole family involved. While Mom and Dad are tending to the fire or preparing the main course, the kids can be setting up the camp table, arranging beverages or working on the side dishes. You'll be surprised how keen people are to pitch in and help when the reward is enjoying a tasty meal in the fresh air.

1 French baguette
1/2 cup (125 mL) herb and garlic cream cheese
1/2 cup (125 mL) chopped sun-dried tomatoes in oil
1 cup (250 mL) shredded part-skim mozzarella cheese

Prepare campfire, or preheat grill to medium. Slice baguette in half lengthwise. Spread cream cheese evenly over 1 cut side. Sprinkle with tomatoes and mozzarella cheese. Top with remaining baguette half and press together. Wrap in foil. Heat on grill for about 10 minutes, turning once.

Teriyaki Steak

(*see* photo p. 52)

Serves 6 to 8

Perhaps the most exciting and traditional meal to serve outdoors on the open fire is the great Canadian beef steak. A good cut of sirloin served with this teriyaki recipe will make you feel like you have died and gone to heaven! Keep a close eye on the temperature when cooking leaner cuts of beef such as sirloin. In my experience, less marbled meats require a lower heat than, say, rib grilling steaks.

> 1 cup (250 mL) teriyaki (or soy) sauce
> 1/2 cup (125 mL) lemon juice
> 3 Tbsp (45 mL) honey
> 2 tsp (10 mL) garlic powder
> 3 × 1 lb (454 g) beef sirloin steaks

Mix teriyaki sauce, lemon juice, honey and garlic powder in small bowl. Place steaks in sealable plastic bag and pour in marinade. Let sit in cooler or refrigerator for at least 6 hours.

Prepare campfire, or preheat grill to medium-high. Remove steaks from marinade, and discard marinade. Grill steaks for about 10 minutes per side, flipping no more than twice, until steak is medium on inside. Place steak on cutting board and cut into 1-inch (2.5 cm) thick slices. Serve with your choice of side, such as baked potato and garden salad.

Try with This  **Corn Relish**

Makes 2 cups (500 mL)

1 × 12 oz (341 mL) can kernel corn, drained
1/2 cup (125 mL) chili sauce
3 Tbsp (45 mL) minced onion
2 Tbsp (30mL) brown sugar
1 Tbsp (15 mL) vegetable oil
1 Tbsp (15 mL) white-wine vinegar

Combine all ingredients in small pot and bring to boil. Simmer for 5 minutes. Let cool. Cover and place in cooler or refrigerator.

Camp Stove Beef Stroganoff

Serves 4

There is just something about the great outdoors that seems to invoke a large appetite and the need to eat protein-rich meals like this one. My guess is that it has to do with the body's reaction to the combination of fresh air and outdoor physical activity. Hearty meals fit right in when camping or relaxing outdoors.

3/4 lb (340 g) beef sirloin steak, cut into strips
1 large onion, sliced
1 cup (250 mL) sliced mushrooms

2 cups (500 mL) beef broth
1 cup (250 mL) water
1 × 10 oz (284 mL) can condensed cream of chicken soup
2 1/2 cups (625 mL) medium egg noodles
1 Tbsp (15 mL) Worcestershire sauce
1/4 tsp (1 mL) pepper

3/4 cup (175 mL) sour cream

Prepare campfire, or preheat grill to medium. In skillet, fry beef until browned, stirring often to avoid sticking. Remove beef to separate bowl. Add onion and mushrooms to skillet and cook for 3 minutes. Add to beef in bowl. Set aside.

Combine broth, water and soup in skillet. Bring to a boil and add egg noodles. Cook at a gentle boil, stirring often, until noodles are tender. Add Worcestershire sauce and pepper. Simmer for 5 minutes.

Return beef mixture to skillet to heat gently. Stir in sour cream and heat, but do not boil. Serve and enjoy!

Malaysian Brochettes

(*see* photo p. 69)

Serves 4 to 6

Soaking wooden skewers is something most people forget to do, but it is an important task, especially when cooking on an outdoor heat source. Most experts suggest soaking skewers in water for at least 30 minutes but no more than 2 hours, because they become too soft. For those who find soaking skewers too tedious, opt for metal skewers instead. I have found that square- or triangular-shaped skewers work much better than the traditional rounded ones—they hold the meat and vegetables more securely so that the food doesn't spin around as you turn the skewers on the grill.

1/2 cup (125 mL) soy sauce
2 Tbsp (30 mL) honey
2 Tbsp (30 mL) lime juice
1 Tbsp (15 mL) curry powder
1 Tbsp (15 mL) chili powder
1 medium onion, minced
2 garlic cloves, minced

1 1/2 lbs (680 g) beef sirloin, cut into 1-inch (2.5 cm) cubes

In medium bowl, add all ingredients except beef and mix well. Add beef and marinate in cooler or refrigerator for 10 to 12 hours.

Soak wooden skewers in water for 30 minutes (or use metal skewers). Prepare campfire, or preheat grill to medium. Remove beef from marinade, and discard marinade. Thread meat cubes onto pre-soaked wooden skewers (or metal skewers). Cook skewers for about 8 minutes until beef is slightly pink (and hot) in centre.

Try with This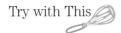

Fried Green Tomatoes
Serves 4

2 Tbsp (30 mL) olive oil
3 green tomatoes
1/2 tsp (2 mL) salt
1/2 tsp (2 mL) pepper
1/4 cup (60 mL) milk
1/2 cup (125 mL) flour
2 eggs, beaten
2/3 cup (150 mL) breadcrumbs

Prepare campfire, or preheat grill to medium. Heat oil in skillet. Cut tomatoes into slices about 1/2 inch (12 mm) thick and season with salt and pepper. Place milk, flour, eggs and breadcrumbs in 4 separate shallow bowls. Dip tomato slices individually in milk, then in flour, then in eggs and finally in breadcrumbs. Fry tomato slices in skillet for about 5 minutes on each side until brown.

Rotisserie Pepper Roast

Serves 10 to 12

Using a rotisserie in the outdoors can be a bit tricky when it is not attached to a gas barbecue. Manual rotisseries are available commercially, or you could make your own (*see* p. 7). Rotisseries enable you to cook such things as a roast of beef over the coals of an open fire. Every summer back home at the Masonic picnic, we cooked an entire pig (and occasionally a side of beef) on a large rotisserie known by the French word *méchoui*. These large rotisserie gatherings or *méchouis* are extremely popular in many parts of Québec and have become a summertime tradition. Take it from someone who has enjoyed many a *méchoui*—they are an outdoor cooking event you will want to be a part of!

> 2 Tbsp (30 mL) Dijon mustard
> 1 Tbsp (15 mL) lemon juice
> 1 Tbsp (15 mL) crushed peppercorns
> 1/2 tsp (2 mL) dried oregano
>
> 1 × 3 to 5 lb (1.4 to 2.3 kg) beef sirloin tip roast
>   (or round or rump roast)

In medium bowl, combine all ingredients except roast. Rub mixture over roast and let stand in cooler or refrigerator for at least 1 hour.

Prepare campfire, or preheat grill to medium. Place roast on rotisserie. On indirect heat, cook for about 25 minutes per pound for medium doneness. Serve with Carrot Salad, p. 137.

London Broil

Serves 6

For people who are not seasoned campers and who do not hunt, fish or regularly spend any time in the great outdoors, finding activities to keep occupied outdoors may seem like a daunting task. In this day and age, however, what is now referred to as "eco-tourism" is becoming a growing recreational activity across the country. It is generally geared toward people who wouldn't normally travel the woods and water in their spare time. Enjoying such things as walking a backwoods trail or observing nature firsthand can be very fulfilling to those who spend most of their time in the concrete jungle.

1/3 cup (75 mL) vegetable oil
1/3 cup (75 mL) vinegar
3 Tbsp (45 mL) brown sugar
3 Tbsp (45 mL) soy sauce
2 medium onions, sliced
1 garlic clove, crushed
1/2 tsp (2 mL) pepper

1 1/2 lbs (680 g) beef flank steak

In medium bowl, combine all ingredients except beef. Place beef in marinade. Cover and put in cooler or refrigerator for at least 4 hours.

Prepare campfire, or preheat grill to medium. Remove beef and onions from marinade, and discard marinade. Cook beef for about 10 minutes, turning once, until slightly pink (and hot) in centre. Cook onions in skillet until warm. Cut beef diagonally across grain into very thin slices. Serve beef slices drizzled with onions.

Smoked Prime Rib

Serves 8

If you are new to smoking meat, I suggest doing your research before you get into it and maybe joining a meat-smoking forum. Basically, there are three schools of thought for how best to smoke meat outdoors: the traditional charcoal and wood smoker, the electric smoker and the propane barbecue smoker. The type of smoker used really has more to do with the location you're in and how portable you need your smoker to be. Obviously, if you plan on smoking meat in a remote outdoor setting, an electric meat smoker is not an option, and large propane barbecue smokers may not be convenient. From a taste standpoint, the final product remains about the same with a variety of different smoker types. Smoking is a delicious way to enjoy beef, pork, chicken, fish or a number of different wild game meats.

2 Tbsp (30 mL) seasoning salt
2 Tbsp (30 mL) paprika
2 Tbsp (30 mL) salt
2 Tbsp (30 mL) black pepper
2 Tbsp (30 mL) white pepper
1 Tbsp (15 mL) brown sugar
1 Tbsp (15 mL) cayenne pepper

1 × 6 lb (2.7 kg) prime rib roast

Soak wood chips for 1 to 2 hours (*see* Tip). Preheat smoker to 250°F (120°C). Combine all ingredients except roast and mix well. Rub mix all over roast. Place roast in cooking chamber, close lid and cook. After about 2 hours, test meat temperature with meat thermometer. Internal temperature should be 145°F (63°C) for medium-rare, 160°F (71°C) for medium or 170°F (77°C) for well done. Once meat has reached desired doneness, remove from smoker, rest for 5 minutes and serve.

 USING WOOD CHIPS WHEN SMOKING

You may use dry wood chips when soaking meat, but soaked chips provide more smoke and better flavouring. Soak wood chips for 1 to 2 hours.

Apricot-glazed Veal Cutlets

Serves 6

One complaint I sometimes hear about cooking outdoors is the work involved in packing all the ingredients. My wife, Cheryl, has found a way to streamline this process: she plans meals in advance and measures dry ingredients for each dish in a sealed container or sealable plastic bag. With such planning, you will have all your ingredients measured and ready to go. Another trick we sometimes use is to precook our side dishes. You can often precook or partially precook such sides as rice or potatoes, thus saving time when you hit the woods and need to focus on your main course.

1/2 cup (125 mL) apricot jam
2 tsp (10 mL) lemon juice
1 tsp (5 mL) thyme
6 veal cutlets, 1/2 to 3/4 inch (1.25 to 2 cm) thick

1 bunch shallots, thinly sliced

Combine jam, lemon juice and thyme in medium bowl. In sealable plastic bag, spread mixture over veal. Place in cooler or refrigerator for 3 hours.

Prepare campfire, or preheat barbecue to medium. Spray cooking grid with non-stick cooking spray. Grill veal for 5 to 10 minutes per side until meat is done to medium and centre is pink. Serve veal over bed of shallots.

Horseradish Burgers

Serves 6

When did you enjoy your most memorable outdoor burger? For me, it was during a fishing trip to Mistassini Lake in June 1994. I will never forget the burgers my father, my brothers-in-law and I ate that night, prepared by Sy Holtz and his son Jimmy of Pittsfield, Maine. Jimmy operated a beef farm and brought some incredible hamburger meat along with him. To this day, I don't know what he put in those burgers or how he prepared them, but they were the best hamburgers I have ever had. My father tells me it had more to do with eating them in the beautiful northern Québec landscape. Perhaps it is true that food cooked outdoors just tastes better.

> 2 lbs (900 g) ground beef
> 2 Tbsp (30 mL) horseradish
> 1 carrot, grated
> 1 medium onion, finely chopped
> 1/2 cup (125 mL) Golden Italian dressing
> 1 1/2 cups (375 mL) breadcrumbs
> 1 egg
>
> 6 hamburger buns

Prepare campfire, or preheat grill to medium. Combine all ingredients except buns in large bowl. Form into 6 hamburger patties. Grill for about 10 minutes, turning regularly, until no longer pink. Serve on buns.

Try with This 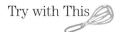 **Grilled Onions**

(*see* photo p. 88)

Serves 4 to 6

1/2 tsp (2 mL) balsamic vinegar
3 Tbsp (45 mL) warmed honey
1 1/2 Tbsp (25 mL) soy sauce
3 large onions
olive oil for basting

Prepare campfire, or preheat grill to high. In small bowl, combine vinegar, honey and soy sauce. Mix well. Peel and cut onions into slices about 1/2 inch (12 mm) thick; keep slices from falling into rings. Baste onion slices with olive oil and place on grid for about 15 minutes, turning and basting frequently, until onions are very tender. Brush with honey mixture and leave on grill for 1 to 2 minutes to heat thoroughly. Remove and serve.

Spicy Hot Burgers

(see photo p. 70)

Serves 4

When spending time in the great outdoors, the equipment you choose can often make or break your trip. Several years ago, I had the good fortune of running into Dave Cook, a camping equipment designer. Dave, an avid camper himself, designed his equipment tough enough to withstand the rigours of the Pacific Northwest. His camp tables are made of select grade laminated wood, covered with a water-resistant fabric. He also developed a camp bed that truly is a breath of fresh air compared with the spine-benders I've used in the past. Trust me—having quality camping equipment will make all the difference when enjoying time afield.

1 lb (454 g) medium ground beef
1/4 cup (60 mL) finely chopped red onion
2 garlic cloves, crushed
1/2 tsp (2 mL) pepper
1 Tbsp (15 mL) chopped parsley
1/4 tsp (1 mL) dried chili flakes

2 red peppers, cut into rings
4 slices processed cheese
4 hamburger buns
olive oil, for brushing buns
lettuce

Mix ground beef, onion, garlic, pepper, parsley and chili flakes. Shape mixture into 4 patties. Cover and place in cooler or refrigerator for 2 to 3 hours (*see* Tip).

Prepare campfire, or preheat grill to medium. Place patties and pepper rings on grill beside one another and grill for 8 to 12 minutes, flipping not more than twice, until burgers are done. Place slice of cheese on each patty for 1 minute before cooking is completed. Brush buns with olive oil and place face-down on grill until lightly toasted.

Place lettuce and burgers on buns, and top with pepper rings.

 MAKE BEFORE LEAVING

When you're cooking outdoors, it may be easier to prepare the burgers at home in advance, place them in a sealed container and bring them with you in a cooler.

Foggy Lake Beans

Serves 6

Perhaps it's just that hilarious scene from the old movie *Blazing Saddles*, but it seems there has always been some connection between eating beans and sitting around an open fire. My teenage camping trips were not complete without a trusty can of Libby's Beans. Granted, it was not a fancy meal, but there was just something special about sitting along the shore of Foggy Lake, Québec, eating beans. My friends and I even started forgetting our utensils so we could fashion our own spoons from sticks of wood. Eating beans brings back visions of whittled spoons, a small outdoor cooking fire and good friends gathered around. This updated version of Foggy Lake Beans brings me back to a simpler day every time I cook it. How often can you say that about a meal?

2 lbs (900 g) ground beef or venison

1 onion, chopped
2 Tbsp (30 mL) chili powder
1 × 15 oz (425 mL) can tomato sauce
1 × 15 oz (425 mL) can crushed tomatoes
1 × 15 oz (425 mL) can kidney beans
1/2 tsp (2 mL) minced garlic
2 cups (500 mL) water

1/2 tsp (2 mL) salt
1/2 tsp (2 mL) pepper
chopped onion for garnish

Prepare campfire, or preheat grill to medium-high (*see* Tip). Cook meat in skillet until brown. Transfer to large pot or Dutch oven; add chopped onion, chili powder, tomato sauce, crushed tomatoes, kidney beans, garlic and water. Bring to a simmer and cook for about 1 hour, stirring frequently. Add salt and pepper, and top with onion.

 COOKING ON COALS

If you're cooking directly on coals, keep a close eye on the pot so the beans do not stick. You will need a strong campfire to maintain a medium-high heat for at least 1 hour.

Sloppy Joes in the Great Outdoors

Serves 8

Cooking and preparing meals outdoors requires a certain frame of mind. When doing it for the first time, many people find it difficult compared with cooking at home in the comfort of their own kitchens. But once they relax and learn a few tricks of the trade, it becomes easier. Once you become adept at building your own campfire to produce a bed of hot coals, this recipe is an easy choice that everybody enjoys—even the children will come back with clean plates.

8 strips bacon

1 medium onion, diced
2 lbs (900 g) ground beef
1 × 6 oz (170 mL) can tomato paste
1 × 10 oz (284 mL) can condensed tomato soup
1 red pepper, diced

Prepare campfire. Cook bacon in cast-iron skillet over hot coals. Transfer bacon to paper towels to drain; crumble or cut into small chunks. Drain grease.

Add onion to skillet. Brown slightly. Add ground beef and brown. Add tomato paste, tomato soup, red pepper and bacon. Simmer for 30 minutes, stirring occasionally to keep ingredients from sticking. Serve with white bread or homemade bannock (*see* Old-fashioned Campfire Bannock, p. 10).

BBQ Sausage Burgers

Serves 4

BBQ Sausage Burgers put an interesting spin on the average burger and are sure to be a hit. I regularly try new ingredients when preparing burgers for my camping trips. Since eating hamburgers and spending time outdoors have always gone perfectly together, whip up a batch of these BBQ Sausage Burgers and see if your guests appreciate the added bite. My guess is they will.

1/2 lb (225 g) lean ground beef
1/2 lb (225 g) ground sausage
1/4 cup (60 mL) hot sauce
1 egg
1 cup (250 mL) Italian breadcrumbs

4 slices mozzarella cheese
1/2 cup (125 mL) your favourite barbecue sauce
hamburger buns

Prepare campfire, or preheat grill to high. In medium bowl, combine beef, sausage, hot sauce and egg. Combine mixture with your hands. Add breadcrumbs slowly until mixture holds together well. Divide mixture into 4 equal portions and form into balls. Flatten into burger shapes, about 1/4 inch (6 mm) thick.

Arrange burgers on grill and cook for 15 to 20 minutes, turning once. Just before removing from heat, place a slice of cheese on each burger. Remove from heat and serve on hamburger buns with barbecue sauce.

Try with This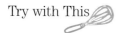

Sweet Mustard Barbecue Sauce

Makes 2 cups (500 mL)

1/4 tsp (1 mL) ground oregano
1/4 tsp (1 mL) pepper
1/4 tsp (1 mL) cayenne pepper
1/4 cup (60 mL) cider vinegar
1 cup (250 mL) prepared mustard
1/2 cup (125 mL) molasses
1/4 cup (60 mL) honey
1 tsp (5 mL) oil

Prepare campfire. Combine oregano, pepper and cayenne pepper in cast-iron skillet. Add vinegar slowly, and mix well. Place skillet over hot coals and add remaining ingredients. Bring to a boil, stirring constantly. Lift skillet to about 6 inches (15 cm) away from coals and simmer for 10 minutes, stirring occasionally.

Hot Campfire Chicken Wings (p. 8)

Forked-stick Ham and Cheese (p. 18)

Cheryl's Hearty Chili

(see photo p. 87)

Serves 6

Cheryl's Hearty Chili is the perfect meal for those cooler evenings around camp. There aren't too many people who don't enjoy this recipe. Campfire control is of utmost importance here, but once you have mastered that, it is all about the simmering time. The recipe calls for a Dutch oven over the campfire, but can just as easily be done over a Coleman or propane camp stove under inclement weather. We always serve Cheryl's Hearty Chili with a fresh loaf of crusty bread from the local bakery down the road.

1 lb (454 g) lean ground beef
1 cup (250 mL) chopped onion
2 garlic cloves, finely chopped

2 1/2 cups (625 mL) chunky salsa
1 × 4 oz (114 mL) can diced green chilies
2 tsp (10 mL) chili powder
1/2 tsp (2 mL) ground cumin
2 × 14 oz (398 mL) cans red kidney beans, rinsed and drained

Prepare campfire. In Dutch oven, sauté ground beef, onion and garlic until nicely browned. Drain off fat. Add salsa, chilies, chili powder and cumin. Add kidney beans and bring to a boil. Reduce heat to low and cover. Cook for about 30 minutes.

Try with This  **Campfire Fried Bread**
Serves 6

3 cups (750 mL) vegetable oil
2 cups (500 mL) flour
1 tsp (5 mL) baking powder
1 tsp (5 mL) salt
1 Tbsp (15 mL) shortening
3/4 cup (175 mL) water

Prepare campfire, or preheat grill to medium. Heat oil in large cast-iron skillet or Dutch oven. Mix flour, baking powder and salt in medium bowl. Work in shortening, then add water and mix well. Shape into 6 balls of equal size. Roll 1 ball of dough at a time to 1/8 inch (3 mm) thick; cut each into 6 wedges. Fry in hot oil until golden brown and slightly swollen.

Solar Oven Chili

Serves 10

The most common solar oven today is a solar box cooker, available commercially, which is capable of reaching temperatures of about 300°F (150°C). However, even with the best-quality solar box cooker, your meal will need to cook much longer than in a conventional oven. But meals such as this chili can be effectively cooked as long as there is proper planning. It is best to start cooking before noon when the sun is high; this timing also gives you several hours of daylight in which to have your meal prepared from start to finish. It may seem like a lot of work, but the satisfaction of cooking dinner in the most environmentally friendly way possible is just great. Trust me—your unorthodox cooking method will be one heck of a conversation piece during dinner hour.

1 × 12 oz (341 mL) can kidney beans
1 × 12 oz (341 mL) can red beans
3 × 12 oz (341 mL) cans diced tomatoes, drained
1 × 12 oz (341 mL) can diced green chilies, drained
1 onion, finely chopped
2 garlic cloves, minced
1 package chili mix
1/2 tsp (2 mL) pepper
1 tsp (5 mL) dried oregano
1 Tbsp (15 mL) salt
2 beef bouillon cubes, dissolved in small amount of water

Drain and rinse kidney beans and red beans. Place beans in large pot with remaining ingredients and stir. Place in solar oven and cook for 3 to 6 hours—the longer, the better.

Lasagna in a Dutch Oven

Serves 6

This recipe is sure to become a family favourite. As with many Dutch oven dishes, this lasagna can easily be done on a camp stove as well as over the open coals. You will need a thick bed of coals to cook this properly from beginning to end, just as with most open-fire casserole meals. One trick I have learned over the years is to be prepared well in advance, which may entail building a fire as much as 1 hour ahead of time if you have to. The biggest mistake most campers make is to look at their watch and say, "Okay, it's 5:00, time to start working on dinner!" If a campfire is your only cooking area, and you have not started putting together the recipe ingredients for this meal or started the fire by 5:00 PM, you will not be eating for at least three hours and will soon have several hungry (and grouchy) campers on your hands.

1 1/2 lbs (680 g) lean ground beef
1 × 26 oz (737 mL) can pasta sauce

3 eggs
2 1/4 cups (550 mL) cottage cheese
1/4 cup (60 mL) grated Parmesan cheese
1 cup (250 mL) shredded mozzarella cheese, *divided*

12 oven-ready lasagna noodles

Prepare campfire, or preheat grill to medium. Brown ground beef in Dutch oven. Drain beef and transfer to bowl. Mix in pasta sauce and set aside. In separate bowl, combine eggs, cottage cheese, Parmesan cheese and 1/2 cup (125 mL) mozzarella cheese.

Break up 4 lasagna noodles and place on bottom of Dutch oven. Next, put half of ground beef mixture on top of noodles. Layer half of cheese mixture over top, then another 4 broken-up lasagna noodles. Repeat layers until final topping of lasagna noodles. Top with 1/2 cup (125 mL) mozzarella cheese. Cook for 30 to 45 minutes until noodles are tender and lasagna is hot. Let stand for 5 minutes before serving.

Sweet and Sour Meatballs

Serves 6

Being the gadget and safety buff that I am, I sometimes go overboard when it comes to high-tech devices. The handheld GPS unit, however, is one gadget I will never be without. When most people think of GPS units, what automatically come to mind are those things in our vehicles that tell us which way to turn. A handheld GPS, though basically the same technology, is a bit more sophisticated than that. The Magellan handheld I use is installed with a high-detail map database and is accurate to within a couple of metres on the ground. The real beauty of a handheld is the ability to set what are called "waypoints." It is like sticking a pin in a topographic map, so you can always return to that spot with ease. When I travel in the outdoors, especially unknown territory, I always set a series of waypoints to serve as geographical reference. Some good waypoints to set on your GPS would be the location of your tent, a canoe portage trail, the spot where your vehicle is parked and perhaps the location of the park office. If you plan to do any remote camping this summer, I suggest you take a GPS and mapping course. It could very well save your life.

1 × 14 oz (398 mL) can jellied cranberry sauce
1 × 12 oz (341 mL) bottle chili sauce
1 × 3 lb (1.4 kg) box pre-made frozen meatballs

Prepare campfire, or preheat grill to low. In Dutch oven, combine cranberry sauce and chili sauce. Mix well and simmer until smooth. Add meatballs, mix well and allow to simmer for 30 minutes, stirring occasionally.

Wilderness Stew

Serves 4 to 6

I have enjoyed wilderness stew more times than I can remember, and it has always been the traditional meal for the first evening at our deer camp. The great thing about this recipe is its flexibility for preparation and eating. The vegetables and even the stewing beef can be prepared in advance and simmered once you get to your campsite, or if you prefer, you can make it fresh on the spot once you arrive in the great outdoors. I often substitute the stewing beef with venison. A wild game meat adds a certain outdoorsy feel to this already great dish. The best part about Wilderness Stew is that the flavour improves when you reheat it, so be sure to save enough in the pot for a second meal!

2 Tbsp (30 mL) vegetable oil
2 lbs (900 g) stewing beef
1 medium onion, sliced
3 cups (750 mL) water
1 tsp (5 mL) garlic powder
1/2 tsp (2 mL) salt
1/2 tsp (2 mL) pepper

1/2 cup (125 mL) sliced celery
1/2 cup (125 mL) sliced turnip
5 medium potatoes, quartered
1/2 cup (125 mL) flour (if necessary)

In medium skillet over medium, heat vegetable oil (*see* Tip). Add beef and sauté until slightly browned. Add onion, water, garlic powder, salt and pepper, and cook until onion is soft.

Place beef mixture in large stewing pot. Add vegetables and simmer, covered, for at least 2 hours until vegetables have softened. Stir from time to time to keep from sticking. Add flour to thicken before serving if necessary. Serve with fresh bread or Old-fashioned Campfire Bannock, p. 10.

 COOKING STEWS

Wilderness Stew and many other stews are best cooked on a camp stove to allow ample simmering time.

Campfire Stew

Serves 8

Whenever you're cooking around hot coals, remember that safety always comes first. Outdoor fires burn hot and bright, and since there's copious oxygen in and around the fire, a fire can become a hazard if you're not careful. Never wear loose-fitting clothes around the fire and avoid things like sweaters draped over your shoulder or material that could accidentally catch a spark or open flame. My own children love to be around the campfire, but my wife and I always keep a close eye on them so they don't get too close. Unfortunately, many people's cooking fires tend to be too large for no reason. Make a small fire so you can sit up close!

1/2 cup (125 mL) flour
1 tsp (5 mL) salt
1 tsp (5 mL) sugar
3 lbs (1.4 kg) stewing beef

1 × 14 oz (398 mL) can beef broth
1/2 tsp (2 mL) fresh thyme leaves
1/4 tsp (1 mL) pepper
1/4 tsp (1 mL) garlic powder
1/4 tsp (1 mL) rosemary
2 cups (500 mL) peeled and cubed turnip
4 potatoes, peeled and cubed
3 large carrots, peeled and thinly sliced

Prepare campfire. Combine flour, salt and sugar in sealable bag and shake well to mix. Add beef to bag. Shake again to coat beef well. Remove beef from bag and discard excess flour mixture. Pour beef broth into large stew pot and add beef and remaining ingredients. Place stew pot over centre of hot coals. Cook for about 2 hours, stirring occasionally to prevent sticking, until meat is done.

Bison Steaks

(*see* photo p. 88)

Serves 8

Bison meat is a great alternative to beef because of its natural properties and nutritional value. It is low in fat, low in cholesterol and, best of all, low in calories. The other great thing about bison is the natural way it is commercially farmed, compared with beef cattle. Bison are typically raised without the use of growth hormones, antibiotics and animal by-products, additives more commonly used in the beef industry. I would describe bison as being very much venison-like but without the strong gamey flavour. Bison offers a great change of pace when you're looking for a new recipe for the grill this summer.

1 Tbsp (15 mL) black peppercorn
1 tsp (5 mL) dill seed
4 tsp (20 mL) salt
2 tsp (10 mL) paprika
2 tsp (10 mL) hot pepper flakes
1 tsp (5 mL) garlic powder

4 × 14 to 16 oz (396 to 454 g) bison rib steaks
4 tsp (20 mL) extra-virgin olive oil

Prepare campfire, or preheat grill to high. In small bowl, combine peppercorn and dill seed and grind together. Add salt, paprika, pepper flakes and garlic powder. Rub each steak with 1 tsp (5 mL) oil and sprinkle with rub mixture.

Place steaks on grill and cook, covered, for 6 to 8 minutes, turning once, until slightly pink (and hot) in centre.

Barbecued Bullwinkle

Serves 4

Many people consider moose meat, regardless of how it is cooked, the king of wild red meats! Once you get past the idea of eating wild game, you will find that moose is every bit as good as beef and a whole lot healthier. For those of you who have never tried moose, you will be surprised to learn how flavourful and similar to beef it is. In my experience, moose tends to be more tender and less stringy than some cuts of beef and is typically a lot milder than other wild game meats. Trust me, you will want to invite "the king" to every barbecue!

> 2 Tbsp (30 mL) vinegar
> 1/2 cup (125 mL) olive oil
> 1 garlic clove, crushed
> 1 tsp (5 mL) salt
> 1/2 tsp (2 mL) pepper
>
> 4 × 14 to 16 oz (396 to 454 g) moose steaks
>   (inside round or sirloin)

Mix all ingredients except steaks in small pan and bring to a boil. Cool. Place steaks in shallow baking dish and pour marinade over top; marinate in cooler or refrigerator for at least 3 hours.

Prepare campfire, or preheat grill to medium. Remove steaks from marinade, and discard marinade. Sear steaks on cooking grid over coals or on grill until slightly pink inside. Serve with Scalloped Potatoes, p. 63, or Butternut Squash, p. 132.

Venison Swiss Steak

Serves 4

Venison is perhaps the healthiest and most organic of all red meats. White-tailed deer are self-sustaining and can be found in solid numbers throughout Canada. Deer meat possesses a full-bodied taste and texture that in my opinion is distinctly Canadian. All-natural venison is a fantastic alternative to commercially raised beef and pork. The meat of the white-tailed deer is also almost completely devoid of fat, making it a much healthier source of protein than commercially raised beef.

1 1/2 lbs (680 g) venison steaks (inside round or sirloin)
1 cup (250 mL) flour
salt and pepper

1/4 cup (60 mL) vegetable oil
3 large onions, chopped
1 medium celery rib, chopped
1 cup (250 mL) diced tomato
2 Tbsp (30 mL) Worcestershire sauce

Prepare campfire, or preheat grill to medium-high. Coat steaks in flour and season with salt and pepper. In large cast-iron skillet, heat oil and brown steaks on both sides. Add onion, celery, tomato and Worcestershire sauce. Cook over low, 6 to 8 inches (15 to 20 cm) above coals or on camp stove, for about 1 hour until tender.

Venison Tenderloin

Serves 4

The "back strap" of the white-tailed deer, otherwise known as venison tenderloin, is the most tender cut of meat, just as with beef and pork. However, one thing to keep in mind when grilling venison tenderloin, or any other wild red meat, is not to cook it too quickly or under too high a temperature. Wild meats such as venison, which have minimal fat content, are notoriously more difficult to cook outdoors. It is not impossible though, and a good marinade helps greatly in that regard. Focus more on finesse-style grilling as opposed to the high-heat searing action used for a marbled beef steak. Slow and easy wins the race with wild game every time.

> 1 Tbsp (15 mL) vegetable oil
> 2 tsp (10 mL) Worcestershire sauce
> 1 tsp (5 mL) garlic powder
> 1/2 tsp (2 mL) pepper
>
> 2 lbs (900 g) venison tenderloin, cut into 1-inch (2.5 cm) strips

Mix oil, Worcestershire sauce, garlic powder and pepper in large bowl and add tenderloin strips. Make sure strips are covered completely. Cover and place in cooler or refrigerator overnight.

Prepare campfire, or preheat grill to medium, not any higher. Remove strips from marinade, and discard marinade. Cook strips slowly, making sure to turn often, until firm on outside and slightly pink in centre. Serve with Vegetarian Rice, p. 76, or Campfire Skillet Potatoes, p. 131.

Try with This  ## Sautéed Mushrooms

Serves 6

1 lb (454 g) mushrooms
1 cup (250 mL) flour
1/4 cup (60 mL) olive oil
1/4 cup (60 mL) butter

Prepare campfire, or preheat grill to medium. Wash mushrooms well. Place flour in bowl and roll mushrooms in flour to coat. In large cast-iron skillet, heat oil and butter until bubbly. Add flour-coated mushrooms and sauté until light brown.

Plank-grilled Lamb

Serves 4

If you plank cook regularly, make your own planks by purchasing wood at your local lumber or home improvement store. But it's very important to make sure your boards are not chemically treated. A lot of the cedar or alder planks you find at the lumberyard have been treated and are unusable for cooking purposes. Planks should be at least 1/2 inch (12 millimetres) thick and 12 inches (30 centimetres) long. You may want to sand the cooking side with sandpaper before use. Finally, of course, all planks need to be soaked in water for at least 1 hour before "planking" them on the grill. Most recipes call for the cooking surface to be coated with oil before placing the meat. Making your own cedar planks can be an economical way to make plank cooking a regular part of your outdoor cooking repertoire.

1 cedar or applewood cooking plank
1 1/2 lbs (680 g) boneless leg of lamb
1 red pepper

2 Tbsp (30 mL) minced garlic
1 cup (250 mL) chopped shallots
3/4 cup (175 mL) white wine
1/3 cup (75 mL) balsamic vinegar
2 Tbsp (30 mL) Dijon mustard
juice of 1 lemon
1/3 cup (75 mL) olive oil
1 tsp (5 mL) thyme
salt and pepper, to taste

Soak plank in water for 1 hour. Soak wooden skewers in water for 30 minutes (or use metal skewers).

Cut lamb and red pepper into small cubes. In medium bowl, combine remaining ingredients and mix well. Pour mixture over meat and vegetable cubes and marinate in cooler or refrigerator for 3 hours.

Prepare campfire, or preheat grill to medium, and preheat plank. Remove meat and vegetables from marinade, and discard marinade. Alternately thread meat and vegetables onto skewers and place brochettes on hot plank. Cook, covered, until meat is cooked to slightly pink (and hot) in centre. Serve with Mint Sauce, p. 46.

Lamb Chops on the Grid

Serves 4

When looking to purchase an outdoor cooking grid—sometimes called a grate or outdoor grill—there are a few things you should know. There are varying degrees of quality when it comes to portable grilling surfaces, and I'm sure I have used them all over the years. Everyone has their own preferences, but cast-iron or porcelain-coated cast-iron are my favourites. The old-fashioned cast-iron grill is the mainstay of most outdoor cooking, but it does require some maintenance to keep from rusting. A good cleaning, drying and oiling is required after each use. Porcelain-coated cast-iron grills are lower maintenance and generally non-stick and rustproof unless chipped or damaged. If money is no object, stainless-steel grids are the cat's meow for outdoor use. They are great for cooking meats, vegetables and a variety of other dishes, but they come at a premium price. Since the best-tasting food is produced from all-wood fires, choose the grid type you find the most convenient for outdoor cooking. To avoid hassles, though, I suggest you stay away from the cheap steel grids with chrome plating. These low-quality grills are more trouble than they are worth.

> 1/2 cup (125 mL) apple jelly
> 1/4 cup (60 mL) lemon juice
> 1/4 cup (60 mL) brown steak sauce
>
> 8 lamb chops

Prepare campfire, or preheat grill to high. In small bowl, combine jelly, lemon juice and steak sauce and mix well until smooth. Place lamb chops on grill and brush with sauce. Cook for 10 to 12 minutes per side, basting occasionally with sauce, until fully cooked. Serve with any remaining sauce on side.

Try with This  **Mint Sauce**

Makes 1 cup (250 mL)

1/2 cup (125 mL) cider vinegar
1/4 cup (60 mL) confectioner's sugar
1/4 cup (60 mL) fresh mint leaves, rinsed and patted dry

Prepare campfire, or preheat grill to medium. In small saucepan, combine vinegar and sugar. Mix thoroughly and heat, stirring constantly, until sugar is dissolved. Place mint leaves in bowl and pour vinegar mixture over top.

Sweet Honey Pork Chops

Serves 4

When camping and cooking in bear country, safety is always a concern—remember to keep things clean and tidy around camp. Although encounters with black bears and grizzlies are rare, they do occur. Bears are North America's most fearsome omnivores; their sense of smell rivals any animal alive. Don't kid yourself—any bear within 2 and even 3 miles (3 to 5 kilometres) will be able to pick up the scent of your cooking fire within minutes. It is especially important for tent campers to keep their campsites free of garbage. Keep all food products stored in the trunk of your vehicle at night, or suspended by ropes in a tree away from your tent. Let's make sure you don't get any unwanted guests for dinner this summer!

1 × 1 1/2 oz (43 g) envelope onion soup mix
3 Tbsp (45 mL) soy sauce
2 Tbsp (30 mL) honey
2 Tbsp (30 mL) lime juice
1/4 tsp (1 mL) ground ginger

4 boneless pork chops

Blend all ingredients except pork in baking dish. Add pork chops. Cover and marinate in cooler or refrigerator for at least 2 hours, turning pork chops occasionally.

Prepare campfire, or preheat grill to medium-high. Remove chops from marinade, and reserve marinade. Grill pork chops for 15 to 18 minutes, turning once and basting with reserved marinade, until pork is juicy and barely pink in centre.

Mrs. Outdoorsguy's Best-ever Ribs

(*see* photo p. 105)

Serves 4

My wife and I had our wedding reception at my uncle's famous Alfred's Beefeater Steakhouse in Arundel, Québec. Afterward, Uncle Alfie's head chef pulled my wife and I aside to let us in on a few tricks he used in the kitchen. The Beefeater regularly draws a crowd of tourists from nearby Mont Tremblant who are looking to enjoy some of the best food in the Laurentians. Cheryl took Chef Ali's rib recipe and, following some modifications of her own, came up with Mrs. Outdoorsguy's Best-ever Ribs recipe.

2 cups (500 mL) Clamato juice or tomato-clam beverage
1 cup (250 mL) water
4 lbs (1.8 kg) pork back ribs

chicken and rib barbecue sauce (bottled)

Preheat oven to 250°F (120°C). In large, covered roasting pan, add tomato-clam beverage and water to cover bottom of pan. Place ribs on rack inside roasting pan (so that they are not sitting in juices) and cover. Cook in oven for 3 hours. Remove ribs from oven and allow to cool (or meat will fall off the bone and it will be hard to remove from roasting pan). You can make ahead to this point (*see* Tip).

Brush ribs with barbecue sauce.

Preheat grill to medium. Re-coat ribs with barbecue sauce, and place on grill. Cook for 5 minutes per side. Remove from grill and serve.

 MAKE BEFORE LEAVING

> You may "pre-bake" the ribs in the oven at home before you leave on your outdoors excursion, and transport them to your campsite in a sealed container. Then grill as directed in the recipe.

Smoked Pork Tenderloin

Serves 4

As a huge fan of pork tenderloin (aren't we all!), I don't believe there is any wrong way to cook it, but smoking certainly is one of my favourites. This relatively inexpensive "filet mignon" (as compared to beef tenderloin) will simply shine when prepared in an outdoor smoker. I like to watch for fresh pork tenderloin to come on sale and then have it vacuum-packed and frozen for when we plan on heading to the trailer or out on a camping adventure. A small, portable charcoal smoker is about all you need for a few strips of pork tenderloin, and for goodness sake, don't forget your wood chips—they are a crucial part of the smoking process. Smoked pork tenderloin has become one of my family's favourite outdoor meals, and with good reason. It is high in protein and low in fat, and can be served with a variety of tasty side dishes.

1 garlic clove, minced
2 Tbsp (30 mL) teriyaki sauce
2 Tbsp (30 mL) brown sugar
2 tsp (10 mL) white vinegar
1/4 tsp (1 mL) ground ginger
1 Tbsp (15 mL) whole cloves

1 × 1 1/2 to 2 lb (680 g to 900 g) pork tenderloin

In saucepan, combine all ingredients except pork and heat until sugar is dissolved. Place pork tenderloin in sealable plastic bag or bowl; pour marinade over top. Marinate in cooler or refrigerator overnight.

Soak wood chips for 1 to 2 hours.

Remove meat from marinade and place on smoker grill. Pour remaining marinade into smoker's water pan along with 12.7 cups (3 L) of water. Add wood chips to smoker and smoke for 2 to 3 hours. Test doneness with meat thermometer. The internal temperature of pork should be 160°F (70°C). Once meat is thoroughly cooked, remove from smoker and serve.

Smoked Ribs

Serves 2 to 4

I find that most meats come to life when prepared in a smoker, and none are more popular than baby back ribs. Even side ribs do very well in the smoker, but there is just something special about the taste and texture of smoked baby back ribs. I often use the "prebaked" technique from the Mrs. Outdoorsguy's Best-ever Ribs recipe (*see* Tip, p. 48), where they are baked in advance with a layer of Clamato juice and water in a racked roasting pan. Instead of 3 full hours of baking, however, I would do 1 hour here so that the meat does not fall completely off the bone during the smoking process. Ribs smoked this way during a camping trip or at the family cottage mean a meal you will not soon forget.

   1/4 cup (60 mL) honey mustard
   2 Tbsp (30 mL) chili powder
   3 Tbsp (45 mL) paprika
   4 Tbsp (60 mL) brown sugar
   1 Tbsp (15 mL) salt

   2 racks baby back ribs (about 3 lbs [1.4 kg] total)

Soak wood chips for 1 to 2 hours. In bowl, combine all ingredients except ribs and mix well. Rub mixture all over ribs and place in cooler or refrigerator for about 1 hour.

Preheat smoker to 200°F (95°C). Add wood chips and place ribs in cooking chamber. Cook for 2 hours. Remove ribs and wrap in foil. Place ribs in foil back in smoker for another 2 hours. Once cooked, serve and enjoy!

Pie Iron Pizza (p. 19)

Teriyaki Steak (p. 21)
Mother Nature's Grilled Veggies (p. 134)

Grilled Orange Ham Steak

Serves 6

Of all the meats to choose from when camping, ham is not only one of the tastiest but perhaps also the most versatile and easy to handle. In the over three decades I have spent camping in every province in Canada, I cannot recall a single trip where ham of some variety was not served. It stores well and keeps for a long time in a cooler or propane fridge. Regardless whether you prefer bone-in, old-fashioned smoked or toupie-style, ham and camping just seem to go hand-in-hand. And after the ham steaks are cut up for dinner, you will undoubtedly have some leftovers. There is nothing better than ham in the morning with breakfast, fried up in the skillet alongside bacon and sausages, or chunked for use with western omelettes and western sandwiches. If there were one meat voted most outdoor-friendly, ham would have to be it!

1 1/2 cups (375 mL) frozen concentrated orange juice, thawed
1/2 cup (125 mL) cider vinegar
1/2 cup (125 mL) brown sugar
1 tsp (5 mL) mustard powder
1 tsp (5 mL) ginger powder
1 Tbsp (15 mL) molasses
1 Tbsp (15 mL) water

1 × 1 1/2 to 2 lb (680 to 900 g) ham steak, 1 inch (2.5 cm) thick

Prepare campfire, or preheat grill to medium. Place all ingredients except ham in blender and blend until smooth, or whisk together. Place ham steak on grill and brush with sauce. Cook for about 5 to 7 minutes per side, brushing with sauce occasionally, until steak has reached a dark brown colour. Remove from heat and serve with remaining sauce on side.

Dutch Oven Ham and Potatoes Casserole

Serves 4

One of the most memorable ham and potato casseroles I ever had was while we were camping along the shores of Lake Superior near Thunder Bay, Ontario. The thing that I remember most about that trip, besides the ham and potato casserole, is looking out at the vast stretch of water and wondering how far it was to the other side. I truly felt like I was at the ocean, but of course the Great Lakes are much like inland oceans. I have never returned to The Lakehead to camp, but will always remember the feeling of being so close to Lake Superior, the place the First Nations call *Gitchigoomie*, and the sense of being so small. It is wonderful places like Thunder Bay that remind us how vast this great country of ours really is.

1/4 cup (60 mL) butter
1 onion, minced
3 Tbsp (45 mL) flour
2 cups (500 mL) milk
1 1/2 cups (375 mL) diced, cooked ham
3 cups (750 mL) diced potatoes
salt and pepper, to taste
1/2 cup (125 mL) grated Cheddar cheese
2 Tbsp (30 mL) breadcrumbs

Prepare campfire and preheat Dutch oven over coals. Melt butter and add onion. Sauté onion until translucent. Add flour to pot and gradually add milk, stirring constantly until sauce has thickened. Add ham, potatoes and season with salt and pepper. Sprinkle cheese and breadcrumbs on top of mixture. Cook, covered, for 20 to 30 minutes.

Pork Tenderloin Québec-style

Serves 4

Having spent several springs working in a Québec company's syrup operations, I suppose there was little doubt that the delectable maple syrup would find its way into my recipes. Did you know that the province of Québec accounts for 75 percent of the world's production of maple syrup? For whatever reason, the maple trees in *La Belle Province* have what it takes to produce the most perfect liquid known to man. I fondly recall the days of working on the evaporators at the Natural Science School's sugar bush back home in Arundel, Québec. Regardless of how sophisticated a sugar bush is or what sap collection method is used, maple extraction is an extremely labour-intensive business, taking many hours of work to produce a single can of syrup. Having been exposed to the operation from beginning to end, I can fully appreciate Québec maple syrup for what it is.

1 lb (454 g) pork tenderloin

2 Tbsp (30 mL) maple syrup
1 Tbsp (15 mL) Dijon mustard
1 Tbsp (15 mL) lemon juice
1 Tbsp (15 mL) vegetable oil
1 garlic clove, grated
1 tsp (5 mL) dried thyme
1/4 tsp (1 mL) pepper

steak sauce (optional)

Place pork in medium bowl. In small bowl, combine all other ingredients except steak sauce. Mix well, and pour over pork. Cover and place bowl in cooler or refrigerator to marinate for at least 3 hours.

Prepare campfire, or preheat grill to medium. Remove pork from marinade, and reserve marinade. Cook pork for about 20 minutes, brushing occasionally with reserved marinade, until meat is well cooked and no longer pink. Remove from heat and serve with steak sauce on side if desired.

Sausages on the Grill

Serves 4

Since not all outdoor cooking is done on the campfire and many sausages are fried up on portable stoves, it is worth noting that there are some great stoves available on the market today. The three most common types of camp stoves are propane, kerosene and naphtha fuel (or white gas), with propane and naphtha (Coleman) being the most common. The convenience of having a secondary heat source in addition to the open fire gives you the ability to cook under a shelter on those damp, rainy days when making a campfire may not be possible. Most camp stoves feature two burners, one for higher-temperature grilling and a secondary burner for warming or heating. They are portable and typically quite easy to use.

1/4 cup (60 mL) honey mustard
1 tsp (5 mL) cider vinegar
1 large egg yolk
1 Tbsp (15 mL) chopped fresh dill

1 1/2 lbs (680 g) dinner sausages

In small saucepan, combine honey mustard, cider vinegar and egg yolk. Cook over low until thickened. Remove from heat and stir in dill. Set aside to cool.

Prepare campfire, or preheat grill to high. Pierce sausages with a fork and arrange on grill. Cook for 8 to 12 minutes, turning occasionally, until lightly browned. Remove from heat, cut into bite-sized chunks and serve with dip.

Cheryl's Dirty Rice

Serves 4

Every time we plan a trip in the summer to our trailer in the Ottawa Valley, my wife Cheryl pre-arranges the fixings for her famous Dirty Rice. It is a meal the whole family enjoys and has become what you might even describe as a staple of our camping weekends. One trick Cheryl has learned is that it is much easier to measure and portion out all the ingredients in advance at home, and then you are way ahead of the game when dinnertime arrives at camp.

1 bunch shallots, sliced
1 celery rib, chopped
1/2 green pepper, chopped
1 Tbsp (15 mL) butter
2 lbs (900 g) mild sausages, sliced
1 lb (454 g) hot sausages, sliced
2 × 10 oz (284 mL) cans chicken broth
1 × 10 oz (284 mL) water (1 chicken broth can)
2 cups (500 mL) uncooked long grain white rice

Prepare campfire, or preheat grill to medium. Sauté shallots, celery and green pepper in butter in frying pan. In second pan, fry mild and hot sausages. When sausages are cooked, drain off grease. Add vegetables to sausages and stir in remaining ingredients. Bring to a boil and reduce heat to low and simmer for 30 to 40 minutes.

Fresh-air Chicken Pie

Serves 4 to 6

The only thing better than chicken pie is chicken pie served over hot coals. One mistake many outdoor chefs make is rushing the cooking fire. It takes between 1 and 2 hours to produce a bed of hot coals suitable for cooking. If you rush things in the hope that a mediocre-sized bed of coals will suffice, you are sadly mistaken. Prepare your fire well with paper, softwood kindling and a good, dry hardwood base. Allow the fire to burn for long enough that a thick bed of red-hot coals is produced. As I have discovered, taking your time is the key to success.

1 large onion, sliced
1 × 10 oz (284 mL) can sliced mushrooms
2 × 1 lb (454 g) bags frozen mixed vegetables
1 × 10 oz (284 mL) can condensed cream of chicken soup
1/2 cup (125 mL) milk
2 Tbsp (30 mL) olive oil or butter
4 boneless, skinless chicken breasts
1/2 tsp (2 mL) salt
1/2 tsp (2 mL) pepper

Prepare campfire. Coat medium baking pan with non-stick cooking spray and spread onion on bottom of pan. Spread mushrooms and vegetables over onion layer. Mix soup with milk and pour over vegetables. Add olive oil. Season chicken breasts with salt and pepper and lay on top of mixture. Cover pan completely with foil so that no air escapes. Place on cooking grid over hot coals. Check after about 1 hour; cooking time will depend on heat of coals. Cook until chicken is no longer pink inside.

Try with This  **Sugared Baby Carrots**

Serves 4

1 lb (454 g) baby carrots
1/4 cup (60 mL) butter
1/3 cup (75 mL) brown (or yellow) sugar

Prepare campfire, or preheat grill to high. Steam or boil carrots until soft. Drain and place back in pot. Stir in butter and brown sugar, and heat until butter has melted and a nice glaze forms on carrots.

Outdoor Chicken with Vegetables

(*see* photo p. 106)

Serves 6

Cooking over an open fire can be a wonderful, rewarding experience, provided you keep your fire under control. There are several ways to ensure that a small cooking fire remains safe and doesn't turn into a blazing inferno. If you do not have an established fire pit at your disposal, you can build your own with a small shovel and some rocks. Start by digging a 2- to 3-foot (60 to 90 centimetre) hole about 6 inches (15 centimetres) deep. Space out small boulders, about 8 to 12 inches (20 to 30 centimetres) in diameter, around the perimeter of the hole. These simple steps will ensure that your fire doesn't spread, and the rocks will also serve as a solid base for your cooking grid. Always keep in mind that sparks and flying embers are dangerous, so never build an outdoor fire on windy days.

> 6 boneless, skinless chicken breasts
> 6 red potatoes, quartered
> 1/2 lb (225 g) baby carrots
> 2 onions, sliced
> 1 × 12 oz (341 g) can corn
> 2 green peppers, sliced
> 2 cups (500 mL) Golden Italian dressing

Prepare campfire. Divide all ingredients into 2 foil bags (or create your own bags with foil). Fold bags to seal, and place on grid over campfire or on good bed of hot coals. Cook for 35 to 45 minutes per side until potatoes are tender and chicken is no longer pink.

Chicken on a Spit

Serves 4

The really neat thing about Chicken on a Spit is that you can cook it in a barbecue or on the open fire. Using a spit on the campfire will take some setting up, but you will be rewarded with a great-tasting bird! The key to spit-fired chicken is making sure you have coals that are strong enough to last 2 hours or more. A deep bed of hardwood coals is necessary, as is protecting your spit from wind and heat loss. I have found that using 4 good-sized pieces of tin or sheet metal set up to form a wall around the spit helps keep the heat in: a well-dampered fire will last a lot longer than a fire that's open to the elements. Maintaining a nice constant heat is important when using a spit, especially when there is no gas grill around.

1 × 3 to 4 lb (1.4 to 1.8 kg) whole chicken
2 large lemons, cut into chunks
1 cup (250 mL) black or green olives
salt and pepper

Wash chicken under cold water and dry with paper towel. Remove giblets. Place lemons and olives in body cavity and season with salt and pepper. Tie up chicken with wire or kitchen twine.

Prepare campfire, or preheat grill to high. Attach chicken to rotisserie spit and make sure it is centred over heat. Reduce heat to medium-high and cook for about 2 hours until chicken is cooked through. Remove from spit and serve with Scalloped Potatoes, p. 63.

 ROTISSERIE

A rotisserie is a system whereby meat is suspended and rotated above a heat source such as a gas barbecue or campfire grill. Most rotisseries are electric but some are also manual crank-style. Rotisseries are a fabulous way to cook whole chickens because they offer very even heat distribution. Depending on your resourcefulness, if you have any welding experience for example, you could even make your own rotisserie from steel reinforcement bars. The most important components of a rotisserie are a stable attachment device for the meat, often a set of skewers or a metal cage, and a solid stand so that the meat remains a set distance away from the heat source.

Weekend Chicken Brochettes

Serves 8

When cooking chicken or anything else on the campfire, proper wood selection is more important than you may realize. A good campfire requires two very essential ingredients: hardwood "heart wood" and softwood kindling. The hardwood portion of your campfire, be it maple, birch, oak or elm, is the heart and soul of your fire and needs to be completely dry in order to burn properly. Most split hardwood will take at least one year and preferably two years to be dry enough for a good cooking fire. The most popular campfire kindling in Canada is undoubtedly cedar. Cedar, whether it's white or red, will generally take one year to dry after being cut into blocks. Dry wood is the building block for the perfect cooking campfire.

6 boneless, skinless chicken breasts

1 Tbsp (15 mL) grated orange rind
1 Tbsp (15 mL) vegetable oil
2 garlic cloves, minced
1 tsp (5 mL) ground coriander
1 tsp (5 mL) cumin
1/2 tsp (2 mL) salt
1/4 tsp (1 mL) hot pepper flakes
1/4 tsp (1 mL) pepper

Soak wooden skewers in water for 30 minutes (or use metal skewers). Slice chicken into 1- to 2-inch (2.5 to 5 cm) cubes, then thread onto skewers.

Combine all remaining ingredients. Pour into large glass dish. Add chicken skewers and stir to coat. Cover and marinate in cooler or refrigerator for several hours.

Prepare campfire, or preheat grill to medium-high. Place brochettes on greased grill. Close lid or cover and grill, turning skewers regularly, until chicken is no longer pink inside.

Wild Garlic Chicken Burgers

Serves 8

Wild garlic, or wild leeks as they are sometimes called, add a beautiful aroma and flavour to any dish. The bulbs of these naturally occurring plants are generally ripe during the month of May across Canada. Wild garlic grows mostly under old-growth and mature hardwood forest, and can be recognized by its long, dark green leaves. Wild garlic is a plant I often call nature's perfect food because of its rich, full-bodied taste and its ability to be used in many different recipes. Everything from the leaves to the stalk to the succulent bulb is edible, and the distinct flavour is reminiscent of chives or spicy green onion. One thing to remember when picking wild garlic, though, is that you should remove the roots and return them to the soil to ensure future propagation of this important plant species.

1 onion, chopped
2 tsp (10 mL) minced wild (or regular) garlic (*see* Tip)
1 red pepper, chopped
1 cup (250 mL) sliced mushrooms
1 tomato, seeded and chopped
2 carrots, chopped

2 lbs (900 g) ground chicken
1 egg
1/2 cup (125 mL) breadcrumbs
salt and pepper, to taste

8 hamburger buns

Prepare campfire, or preheat grill to medium. Coat skillet with non-stick cooking spray. Sauté onion and garlic until onion has softened. Add red pepper, mushrooms, tomato and carrots and cook to desired tenderness. Set aside and allow to cool completely.

Combine chicken and cooked vegetables in bowl. Add egg, breadcrumbs, salt and pepper and mix well. Form into 8 equal-sized patties. Grill for 5 to 6 minutes per side until done. Serve in hamburger buns with your favorite condiments.

 *tip*   GARLIC FLAVOUR

The flavour will be different depending on whether you use wild or regular garlic.

Summertime Chicken Drumsticks

Serves 4

One issue that many people face when sleeping in the outdoors is making sure that everyone is happy and well fed. Children are often the fussy ones, and finding a meal you can prepare during a wilderness adventure that the kids go for can sometimes be a struggle in itself. Summertime Chicken Drumsticks is one of those campfire meals that adults love, and more importantly, the little ones enjoy as well. On trips such as this, when the kids are happy the parents are happy, so dig in and enjoy!

8 chicken drumsticks

1/3 cup (75 mL) lemon juice
1/3 cup (75 mL) orange juice
1 tsp (5 mL) grated orange rind
1 tsp (5 mL) sesame oil
1 Tbsp (15 mL) olive oil
1 chopped green onion

Rinse chicken under cold water and dry with paper towel. Place chicken in shallow dish. Mix together all remaining ingredients in bowl and pour over chicken. Cover with plastic wrap and place in cooler or refrigerator for several hours or overnight, turning occasionally.

Prepare campfire, or preheat grill to medium. Grease grill. Drain chicken, and reserve marinade. Cook chicken for 15 to 20 minutes, brushing occasionally with reserved marinade, until tender and no longer pink.

Try with This  ## Scalloped Potatoes
Serves 4

1 × 13 1/2 oz (385 mL) can evaporated milk
2 tsp (10 mL) chicken bouillon powder
1 tsp (5 mL) onion powder
4 cups (1 L) peeled, sliced potatoes

Prepare campfire, or preheat grill to medium. In large skillet, heat milk, bouillon powder and onion powder. Stir constantly until smooth. Add potatoes and bring to a boil. Cover and simmer for 30 minutes, stirring regularly, until sauce has thickened and potatoes are soft.

Foil Chicken and Vegetables

Serves 4

While staying at his cottage near Kirkland Lake, Ontario, my friend Matthew decided to cook chicken over the grill of a neglected, old, burnt-out gas barbecue that still had a few ceramic briquettes left on the bottom. He constructed an open-style campfire with twigs and paper on top of the briquettes, then grabbed a container of lighter fluid and poured it over his makeshift fire. He placed the grate directly on top of the ceramic briquettes. The fire got hot enough, and an hour later the chicken was done and he and his family sat down to eat. To their dismay, after the first bite they noticed the chicken tasted awful. Matthew assumed it was just a bad chicken—until he removed the grill and smelled lighter fluid on it. My pal had not allowed the fire to burn off any trace of barbecue starter. It was a good lesson learned, and I have taken it to heart in my own outdoor cooking.

2 cups (500 mL) thinly sliced carrots
2 cups (500 mL) thinly sliced zucchini
4 tsp (20 mL) water

4 boneless, skinless chicken breasts
2 cups (500 mL) chutney
4 tsp (20 mL) curry powder
4 tsp (20 mL) butter

2 cups (500 mL) coconut
2 cups (500 mL) chopped nuts

Prepare campfire, or preheat grill to medium. Tear off 4 pieces of foil about 12 × 14 inches (30 × 36 cm) each and spray with non-stick cooking spray. Divide carrots and zucchini into 4 portions and place in centre of each piece of foil. Put 1 tsp (5 mL) water on top of each.

Place chicken breast on top of vegetables. Mix chutney, curry powder and butter to make paste. Spread on chicken. Sprinkle coconut and chopped nuts on top of each combination. Fold each packet until sealed and place on grill for 15 to 20 minutes until chicken is well cooked and no longer pink in centre.

Beer Can Chicken on the Grill

Serves 4 to 6

I don't necessarily condone alcohol consumption while camping, but if you do plan to bring a few beverages with you, I have discovered certain tricks over the years. I have learned, for example, that canned beer is much more convenient to transport than bottled beer. Cans are lighter, they pack easier and there is no chance broken glass around the campsite will find its way into someone's foot or leg. It is an unwritten rule on any of my adventures afield that bottled beverages are not allowed. If you have cans of beer around, here is a great, easy recipe that is hard to beat when cooking chicken on the grill or barbecue.

1 cup (250 mL) butter, *divided*
2 Tbsp (30 mL) garlic salt, *divided*
2 Tbsp (30 mL) paprika, *divided*

1 × 12 1/2 oz (355 mL) beer
salt and pepper
1 × 3 to 4 lb (1.4 to 1.8 kg) whole chicken

Melt 1/2 cup (125 mL) butter in saucepan. Add 1 Tbsp (15 mL) garlic salt and 1 Tbsp (15 mL) paprika. Set aside.

Prepare campfire, or preheat grill to medium. Take can of beer and discard about half of it (however you see fit), leaving rest in can. Place 1/2 cup (125 mL) butter, 1 Tbsp (15 mL) garlic salt, 1 Tbsp (15 mL) paprika, salt and pepper in beer can. Set chicken on beer can, inserting can carefully into cavity of chicken. Place on disposable baking sheet and baste with prepared butter mixture.

Place baking sheet on grill. Cook over low for about 3 hours until chicken is no longer pink and juices run clear.

Quesadillas on the Grill

(*see* photo p. 123)

Serves 4

First-time campers sometimes have difficulty amusing themselves when cooking outdoors. There are a number of activities you or your kids can do (maybe when Mom and Dad are preparing these quesadillas!). Have you really explored the area around your campsite or that small stream behind the cottage? Ask some fellow campers to join you on a nature walk or maybe take the canoe for a paddle across the lake. Canada is famous for its breathtaking landscapes, and you may be surprised by what you discover in the few minutes before dinner.

> **4 boneless, skinless chicken breasts**
> **squeeze of fresh lime juice**
>
> **4 large flour tortillas**
> **1 × 15 oz (425 mL) bottle salsa**
> **2 to 3 cups (500 to 750 mL) grated Cheddar or mozzarella cheese, or a combination**
> **2 Tbsp (30 mL) chopped shallots**
>
> **guacamole, sour cream and diced red tomato to serve**

Prepare campfire, or preheat grill to medium. Cook chicken until meat is no longer pink and juices run clear. Squeeze a bit of lime juice over chicken and set aside.

Take each tortilla and spread salsa, cheese and shallots on half of each.

Slice chicken into 1/2-inch (12 mm) thick strips and place on tortillas, with strips radiating from middle toward edge. Fold each tortilla in half and place on grill on low—avoid high flames or high heat. After 2 minutes, flip tortillas and grill for another 2 minutes.

Remove tortillas from grill and cut into pie-shaped wedges with pizza cutter. Serve with guacamole, sour cream and tomato.

Sesame Asian Chicken and Vegetables

Serves 4

Sesame Asian Chicken is one of my daughter Emily's favourite recipes when we're spending weekends at our trailer in the Ottawa Valley. After years of camping and cottaging, I have discovered that, to paraphrase from the movie *Field of Dreams*, "if you make good food, they will come." It truly is incredible how a tasty meal served in a beautiful outdoor setting can bring people out of the woodwork and have them coming back for more. Sometimes I'm not sure what the real calling card is. Is it the fresh air and peaceful surroundings, or the smell and taste of a well-cooked meal? I suppose all these elements put together are what keep us coming back to the great outdoors year after year!

4 skinless, boneless chicken breasts

1/4 cup (60 mL) brown sugar
2 Tbsp (30 mL) soy sauce
1 Tbsp (15 mL) minced garlic
1/4 tsp (1 mL) sesame oil
1/8 tsp (0.5 mL) cayenne pepper

1 head broccoli, cut into small pieces
1 onion, cubed
5 large carrots, thinly sliced

Cut chicken into small cubes. In medium bowl, combine brown sugar, soy sauce, garlic, sesame oil and cayenne pepper. Add chicken, broccoli, onion and carrots and toss to coat.

Tear off 4 sheets of heavy-duty foil and place chicken and vegetable mixture in centre of foil pieces. Fold up sides and double-fold top and ends to seal packets.

Prepare campfire, or preheat grill to medium. Cook packets, covered, for about 15 minutes until chicken is done, turning pouches over once while cooking. Serve with Campfire Skillet Potatoes, p. 131.

Grilled Fajitas

Serves 2

When transporting aromatic meats such as chicken or beef in the Canadian wilderness, we should be aware that we are not alone. Large predators and omnivores such as the black bear inhabit most areas of this country and could very well be nearby. By keeping a clean, scent-free campsite and storing food items in our vehicles or hung up in trees away from the campsite at night, we lessen the chance of having an unwanted visitor stop by. Even simple tasks like making sure our cooking grill and campfire are free of food scraps and grease make a huge difference. We don't necessarily need to be paranoid of bear encounters, but being aware that these animals could be nearby and cleaning up after ourselves goes a long way to ensuring our safety.

**2 boneless, skinless chicken breasts
1 onion
1 green pepper**

**2 Tbsp (30 mL) chili powder
1 Tbsp (15 mL) salt
1 Tbsp (15 mL) sugar
1 tsp (5 mL) onion powder
1 tsp (5 mL) garlic powder
1/2 tsp (2 mL) cayenne pepper
1/2 tsp (2 mL) cumin**

**tortilla shells
toppings such as diced tomatoes, sour cream and salsa**

Soak wooden skewers in water for 30 minutes (or use metal skewers). Prepare campfire, or preheat grill to medium.

Cut chicken into 1-inch (2.5 cm) cubes. Cut onion and green pepper to a similar size. In medium bowl, mix chili powder, salt, sugar, onion powder, garlic powder, cayenne and cumin. Roll chicken cubes in mixture.

Alternately thread chicken, pepper and onion on skewers. Grill for about 15 minutes, turning often, until chicken is cooked and no longer pink inside. Remove meat and vegetables from skewers and wrap with tortilla shells. Add toppings such as tomatoes, sour cream and salsa, or whatever your favourite toppings are. Serve and enjoy!

Malaysian Brochettes (p. 22)

Spicy Hot Burger (p. 29)
Sweet Potato Fries (p. 12)

Solar Oven Italian Chicken

Serves 4

Solar cooking, as the name implies, is the art of using energy from the sun
to provide a heat source to cook food. The practice of solar cooking actually
dates back to 1767, when a Swiss physicist, Horace de Saussure, first began
experimenting with the sun's energy. The physicist experimented with what
were known at the time as "hot boxes." He strategically positioned a series of
glass boxes on top of one another in such a way that under each glass box,
the temperature became higher and higher. Saussure's principle remains
somewhat the same today, and there are a wide variety of solar cooking ovens
available commercially that are used to cook food and boil water.

- 4 skinless, boneless chicken breasts
- 1/2 cup (125 mL) Golden Italian dressing
- 1 green pepper, cut into chunks
- 1 tomato, cut into about 6 pieces
- 1 medium onion, cut into chunks

Place chicken breasts into suitable solar roasting pan and pour dressing
over top. Add vegetables and cover. Place in solar oven and cook for at
least 5 hours until chicken is no longer pink. Serve with rice or potatoes.

Try with This 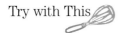 **Siesta Rice**

Serves 6 to 8

1/2 cup (125 mL) water
1 × 10 oz (284 mL) can condensed chicken broth
1/2 cup (125 mL) salsa
2 cups (500 mL) instant rice

Prepare campfire, or preheat grill to medium. In pot, bring water, chicken broth
and salsa to a boil. Stir in rice, cover and remove from heat. Let stand for
5 minutes. Fluff with a fork and serve.

Chicken and Dumplings

Serves 4

If you have never camped in the Canadian Rockies, do yourself a favour and try it sometime. The first time I ever pitched a tent among the largest mountains I had ever seen was with my parents in the early 1980s. Since sleeping and eating in the fresh air was a favourite pastime of mine from a young age, camping in Banff and Jasper was right up my alley. I will never forget that first meal in Banff after a long day of bear-, elk- and bighorn sheep-watching: Chicken and Dumplings done right on the old Coleman stove. I have used naphtha (or white gas) stoves a million times since then, but I will never forget the look and smell of that meal as I sat at a picnic table in one of the most spectacular places on earth. Although cooking Chicken and Dumplings in the heart of the Rocky Mountains is the ultimate treat, it is also a great meal to enjoy in any of this country's fabulous campgrounds!

> **2 × 3 oz (85 g) envelopes chicken noodle soup mix**
> **1 × 12 oz (341 mL) can flaked chicken**
> **1 × 12 oz (341 mL) can corn, peas or carrots (or mixed)**
>
> **1 × 8 oz (226 g) box buttermilk biscuit mix**

In Dutch oven, make soup mixture using only half the water required on package directions. Add chicken and vegetables. Bring to a boil.

Prepare biscuit mix according to package directions and drop spoonfuls into chicken mixture. Cover and simmer for 30 minutes until dumplings are done.

Dutch Oven Chicken Pot Pie

Serves 6

Since there are so many fabulous recipes one can create with a Dutch oven, we like to keep our old yellow Copco Dutchie close by at all times. Sure, the bottom has become blackened over the years, but the enamel-coated cooking area inside is as pristine today as the day we bought it. The only drawback to Dutch ovens, in my opinion, is their size and weight. They are rather heavy, but the options they present while travelling and cooking in the outdoors are limitless.

1/4 cup (60 mL) oil
2 × 12 oz (341 g) cans chicken breast meat
2 tsp (10 mL) minced garlic
1 onion, diced
4 potatoes, diced

3/4 cup (175 mL) milk
1/4 cup (60 mL) flour
2 × 10 oz (284 mL) cans condensed cream of chicken soup
2 tsp (10 mL) poultry seasoning
1 × 15 oz (425 mL) can early peas
1 × 8 oz (226 g) tube refrigerated crescent rolls crescent rolls

Prepare campfire. Heat oil in Dutch oven over hot coals. Add chicken and garlic and cook for about 5 minutes. Add onion and potatoes and cook for about 10 minutes, stirring constantly.

In small cup, mix milk and flour. Add milk mixture, chicken soup, poultry seasoning and peas to Dutch oven. Mix and bring to a boil. Unroll crescent rolls and create dough layer on top of chicken mix. Cover pot and place on coals to bake. Pot pie is ready when top is golden brown and flaky.

Chicken Fingers on the Grill

Serves 4 to 6

Everyone in the Morrison household enjoys chicken strips, and it does not seem to matter what kind they are. However, chicken fingers cooked from scratch with this recipe are a cut above any you will find at the local fast food restaurant. Cooking in the outdoors tends to spoil you for any other kind of cooking.

4 boneless, skinless chicken breasts
salt and pepper

3 Tbsp (45 mL) vegetable oil
2 Tbsp (30 mL) chicken and rib barbecue sauce (bottled)
1 cup (250 mL) cracker crumbs

Soak wooden skewers in water for 30 minutes (or use metal skewers). Prepare campfire, or preheat grill to medium. Cut chicken into 1-inch (2.5 cm) slices about 4 to 5 inches (10 to 12 cm) long. Carefully thread chicken strips onto skewers and sprinkle with salt and pepper.

In bowl, combine vegetable oil and barbecue sauce and mix well. Spread cracker crumbs onto plate. Brush barbecue sauce mixture on chicken skewers and then roll in cracker crumbs. Cook, turning once or twice, until chicken is no longer pink.

Try with This  **Honey Mustard Sauce**
Makes 1 cup (250 mL)

1/2 cup (125 mL) honey
1/2 cup (125 mL) Dijon mustard

In small bowl, combine honey and mustard. Mix well. Great as a dip for chicken strips or a sauce on burgers.

Grilled Cornish Hen

Serves 4

The convenient size of a Cornish hen provides individual portions and adds a touch of class when entertaining. A Cornish hen is essentially a young, immature chicken, bred specifically for harvest at a younger age and weighing no more than 2 pounds (1 kilogram). If you really want to impress your guests this summer, give this Grilled Cornish Hen recipe a try. You will not be disappointed!

1/4 cup (60 mL) lemon juice
3 garlic cloves, pressed
1 Tbsp (15 mL) pepper
1 tsp (5 mL) salt
2 tsp (10 mL) brown sugar
2 tsp (10 mL) grated ginger root
1 1/2 tsp (7 mL) crumbled dried oregano
1/2 tsp (2 mL) ground cumin

4 Cornish hens
1/4 cup (60 mL) extra-virgin olive oil

In small bowl, combine all ingredients, except hens and oil, and mix well. Remove backbone from Cornish hens and separate into halves through middle of breast (*see* Tip). Place hens in large bowl and coat completely with marinade. Let stand in cooler or refrigerator for 1 hour.

Prepare campfire, or preheat grill to medium. Remove hens from marinade, brush with oil and place on grill. Cook for 20 to 25 minutes until juices run clear.

 BUTTERFLYING A CORNISH HEN

Removing the backbone of a Cornish hen, or "butterflying" as some chefs call it, is a simple task, provided you have a good pair of poultry or kitchen shears. Simply place the hen on a wooden cutting board with the back facing upward. Snip the skin along the edge of the backbone from the front of the bird to the back. Turn the hen around and snip along the other side. Once the backbone is exposed, cut through and remove the entire bone. Then push down gently on your hen so as to flatten it slightly. Removing the backbone of a Cornish hen not only gives it a nice, clean appearance, but it also reduces the cooking time.

Asian Grilled Mallard

Serves 2

The first time I ever tried grilled mallard was back in 1990 when I was attending Sir Sandford Fleming College. As part of the Fish and Wildlife Biology program, we participated in fabulous hands-on field camps located in different parts of central and northern Ontario. I will never forget our trip to Loon Lake Camp near Huntsville, Ontario. During that field camp we were not only exposed to several wildlife-management techniques, we were treated to a fabulous wild game dinner as well. We enjoyed grilled goose, mallard duck and wild turkey. It was a toss-up between the wild turkey and the duck for the best-tasting meal, but my money was on the mallard. Kudos to Sir Sandford Fleming College's Frost Campus in Lindsay for running the top-rated Fish and Wildlife program in the country and for serving some of the best mallard I have ever eaten.

> 1/4 cup (60 mL) soy sauce
> 2 Tbsp (30 mL) olive oil
> 1/2 tsp (2 mL) Sriracha (hot Asian chili sauce)
> 2 Tbsp (30 mL) minced garlic
> 1/4 tsp (1 mL) pepper
>
> 4 duck breasts, cut in half

Blend together all ingredients except duck. Add duck breasts and coat well. Marinate for 1 hour in cooler or refrigerator.

Prepare campfire, or preheat grill to medium-high. Remove duck from marinade and discard marinade. Grill duck for 5 to 10 minutes until no longer pink inside.

Try with This  **Vegetarian Rice**

Serves 4

1 cup (250 mL) uncooked long-grain rice
2 1/4 cups (550 mL) water
2 Tbsp (30 mL) onion (or vegetable) soup mix
1/4 tsp (1 mL) salt
1 cup (250 mL) peas
1 cup (250 mL) carrots

Prepare campfire. In saucepan on grid 2 inches (5 cm) over coals, combine rice, water, soup mix and salt, and bring to a boil. Add peas and carrots, and return to a boil. Raise grid to 4 to 6 inches (10 to 15 cm) above coals. Cover and simmer for 12 to 15 minutes until rice and vegetables are tender.

Grilled Canada Goose

Serves 8

Canada geese stand out from other birds in many ways: they are distinctive in their migration patterns, "V" flight formations, and long-necked and long-legged appearance. Even the crazy honking sound they make is unique! The taste of Canada goose is also quite distinctive compared with other wild fowl. Since goose meat is characteristically dark with a high oil content, it does possess a distinctly bold flavour that is sometimes compared to roast beef. As much as you might think that goose has a higher fat and calorie content than is found in duck, you would be wrong. From a nutritional standpoint, 1 cup (250 millilitres) of grilled goose has 425 calories with 30 grams of fat, while 1 cup (250 millilitres) of wild duck has 470 calories with 39 grams of fat.

> 1 whole Canada goose, cleaned and plucked (*see* Tip)
> 4 Tbsp (60 mL) olive oil
> 1 tsp (5 mL) onion powder
> 1 tsp (5 mL) garlic powder
> 1/2 tsp (2 mL) salt
> 1/2 tsp (2 mL) pepper

Prepare campfire, or preheat grill to medium. Cut goose in half down breastbone and coat halves completely with olive oil. Season both halves with onion powder, garlic powder, salt and pepper.

Coat grill with oil or non-stick cooking spray. Place goose halves on grill, skin-side up. Cook each side for 15 to 20 minutes until meat is no longer pink and pulls away easily from breastbone. Remove from grill and let stand for 5 minutes before carving.

 tip   CLEANING AND PLUCKING GOOSE

Pull out all the feathers by hand and discard them. Don't worry about removing the tiny pin feathers—they will quickly singe off and burn on the grill. Tear back the skin on the underside of the bird at the stomach cavity. Remove and discard the entrails, then rinse the goose under cool water and place on paper towel to dry.

Grouse on the Grill

Serves 4

Ruffed grouse, or partridge as many of us still call them, are one of the tastiest upland game birds you will find across North America and are one of the most highly sought-after small game. They are quick and challenging from a sporting standpoint, and extremely mild and flavourful as table fare. With scant fat to keep them "self-basted," they will stick in a pan and dry out quickly if overcooked, so keep that in mind when cooking them.

1/2 onion, finely chopped
1 garlic clove, minced, *divided*
7 Tbsp (105 mL) pomegranate molasses, *divided* (*see* **Tip**)
1 tsp (5 mL) cinnamon
1 tsp (5 mL) cumin
1 tsp (5 mL) lime juice

4 grouse breasts, split in half
salt and pepper, to taste

1 cup (250 mL) diced bacon
1/2 cup (125 mL) whole pistachios

Blend onion, 1/2 garlic clove, 3 Tbsp (45 mL) molasses, cinnamon, cumin and lime juice together in mixing bowl. Season grouse with salt and pepper and place in marinade. Place in cooler or refrigerator for 3 to 4 hours.

Prepare campfire, or preheat grill to medium. Fry bacon in pan until crispy. Drain off all but 1 Tbsp (15 mL) of bacon grease. Remove grouse from marinade, and discard marinade. Add grouse and bacon, 1/2 garlic clove, 4 Tbsp (60 mL) molasses and pistachios to pan and cook on grill until grouse is no longer pink and separates easily from breastbone. Serve with rice and drizzle sauce over top.

 POMEGRANATE MOLASSES

Pomegranate molasses can also be found under the name pomegranate syrup. It is made by reducing the sweet juice of the pomegranate fruit down to a syrupy liquid. In the Middle East, pomegranate molasses is used in a variety of dishes, mostly notably the Turkish rice pilaf. Here in Canada, you will find this ingredient sold in most Middle Eastern or Turkish markets, usually marketed in a 10–12 oz (284–341 mL) bottle, looking very much like traditional molasses in appearance.

Wild Grouse Chili

Serves 4

My old pal Kenny Campbell of Harrington, Québec, is one of the best hunters I have ever known. Over the nearly 40 years Ken and I have been friends, we have camped together more times than I can remember. We have hunted moose in northern Québec and deer in Montebello many times, and he has camped with me probably 100 times or more. He also sure knows his way around a grouse meal! Being an avid partridge (or grouse) hunter, Ken has learned a few tricks for cooking this magnificent feathered creature. Every time I eat grouse, I think of my pal Ken and the many terrific meals we have enjoyed together over the years.

> 3 Tbsp (45 mL) olive oil
> 1 lb (454 g) minced grouse
> 1 red onion, chopped
>
> 1 × 6 oz (170 g) can tomato paste
> 2 cans diced tomatoes, drained
> 1 cup (250 mL) water
> 4 tsp (20 mL) chili powder
> 1/2 tsp (2 mL) each salt
> 1/2 tsp (2 mL) pepper
> 1/2 tsp (2 mL) garlic powder

Prepare campfire, or preheat grill to medium. In cast-iron pan, add olive oil, grouse and onion. Sauté until grouse is brown and onion has softened. Add remaining ingredients and stir. Cover and simmer for 1 to 2 hours until chili has begun to thicken.

Easy Partridge in a Pan

Serves 4

Back in the days when my recreational repertoire included small game hunting, the grouse population fluctuation was as noticeable in the field as it was on the table. There were some years when bird numbers were low. Winters with little snow and bitterly cold temperatures are extremely hard on grouse and partridge, and years with burgeoning predator numbers also have negative effects on small game. There is a well-documented cyclical population pattern between the snowshoe hare and the lynx, running very much like the law of supply and demand. With grouse and partridge, however, the fluctuation in numbers is not so well documented. Ask any wildlife biologist or hunter out there and they will attest to the fact that bird numbers vary greatly from year to year. I recall enjoying far more grouse meals during those years when numbers were high.

3 Tbsp (45 mL) olive oil
1/4 cup (60 mL) flour
1/2 tsp (2 mL) salt
1/2 tsp (2 mL) pepper
6 partridge breasts, halved

Prepare campfire and establish thick bed of coals. Heat olive oil in large cast-iron pan. In medium bowl, mix flour, salt and pepper. Roll partridge pieces in flour. Lay partridge pieces in pan and cook for about 5 minutes on each side until meat is fully cooked.

 Try with This

Campfire Baked Potatoes
Serves 4

4 medium potatoes
1/4 cup (60 mL) butter, softened
toppings as desired, such as cheese, sour cream, chili, sloppy Joes or bacon bits

Prepare some nice hot coals in your campfire. Wash potatoes well and poke several times with a fork. Rub softened butter over each potato, and double wrap with foil. Place potatoes directly on hot coals and cook for 45 to 60 minutes until soft.

Once potatoes have reached desired softness, unwrap carefully—they will be hot—and slice on the top to halfway through. Add toppings such as butter, cheese, sour cream, chili, sloppy Joes, bacon bits or whatever else you have on hand!

Grilled Pheasant

Serves 4

If your children are anything like mine, there is nothing they enjoy more than fresh air. However, when spending time as a family in the outdoors, keeping kids interested throughout an entire camping trip can be half the battle. Finding ways to amuse the little ones can seem difficult until you realize the opportunities that exist around you. It is the duty of parents to share the wonders of nature with their children. When I'm cooking an outdoor meal such as this one, I often take the opportunity to explain a bit about hunting and conservation and how the pheasant came to be part of our dinner. I am proud that my girls understand about enjoying the bounties of nature, and how we must respect and honour rules and regulations when we are spending time in the wilderness.

2 Tbsp (30 mL) olive oil
2 pheasant breasts, cut in half
salt and pepper

Prepare campfire, or preheat grill to high. Heat olive oil in cast-iron pan. Season pheasant breasts with salt and pepper, and place in pan. Cook for about 5 minutes per side until meat is no longer pink. Serve with Asparagus with Almonds, p. 120, or Golden Italian Chef's Salad, p. 139.

Turkey Breast on a Plank

Serves 4

Of all the outdoor cooking methods available today, none have grown as much in popularity in recent years as plank cooking. Plank cooking over open coals has been described as the easy way to smoke different meats without a smoker. The most popular wood for planking is cedar, specifically aromatic red cedar, but other species such as apple, sugar maple, alder and birch have also become quite popular. Avoid wood high in sap content, such as pine: they do not lend themselves well to the planking process. Regardless of which type of plank you choose, outdoor plank cooking will open up a whole new world of cooking opportunities. One caution, though: make sure your plank wood is not pre-treated.

2 cups (500 mL) beer
2 cups (500 mL) water
4 Tbsp (60 mL) honey
1 Tbsp (15 mL) soy sauce
1 Tbsp (15 mL) brown sugar
1 Tbsp (15 mL) olive oil
1 Tbsp (15 mL) pepper
1-inch (2.5 cm) piece fresh ginger, chopped
2 tsp (10 mL) Worcestershire sauce
2 tsp (10 mL) salt

1 × 5 to 6 lb (2.3 to 2.7 kg) turkey breast
1 cedar or applewood cooking plank

In medium bowl, combine all ingredients except turkey and mix well. In plastic container, pour marinade over turkey. Cover and place in cooler or refrigerator overnight.

Prepare campfire, or preheat grill to medium, and preheat cooking plank. Remove turkey from marinade and discard marinade. Cook turkey on plank for about 75 minutes until juices run clear when poked with a fork or skewer.

Smoked Brined Turkey

Serves 10 to 12

For those of you who are tired of the stereotypical dry turkey, brining may be a good option for you. Brining ensures that the meat remains moist even after hours of roasting. The kosher salt works its way through the meat and breaks down proteins, which results in a moist texture after cooking. Some, but not all, brining recipes call for sweet additives to counterbalance the salt infusion, so the choice is yours. The real trick to brining a large turkey in the outdoors is finding a cool space large enough to accommodate such a big pot. I suggest pre-brining your turkey at home before leaving for the woods—that way you only need to pack your meat smoker and wood chips. There is certainly work involved in brining or smoking a turkey, but trust me, you and your guests will be rewarded when this succulent meal hits the picnic table.

> **2 gallons (7.5 L) water**
> **1 1/2 cups (375 mL) kosher salt**
> **2 cups (500 mL) brown sugar**
> **2 Tbsp (30 mL) mild curry powder**
> **2 Tbsp (30 mL) garlic powder**
> **2 Tbsp (30 mL) onion powder**
> **2 Tbsp (30 mL) sage**
>
> **1 × 12 to 14 lb (5.4 to 6.4 kg) whole turkey**

Combine all ingredients except turkey in very large bowl and mix well to make brine. Place turkey in brine, breast down, and refrigerate or place in cool spot for 12 to 14 hours or overnight.

Soak wood chips for 1 to 2 hours. Remove turkey from brine. Discard brine. Rinse turkey inside and out with cold water and pat dry.

Preheat smoker to 250°F (120°C) and place turkey in smoke chamber. Add wood chips and close lid. Test after 4 or 5 hours with meat thermometer. The internal temperature of turkey should be 185°F (85°C) to be cooked thoroughly. Once meat is thoroughly cooked, remove from smoker and serve.

Turkey Drumsticks on the Grill

Serves 4

This popular American meal does not get the attention it deserves in Canada. At the Six Flags Park in Lake George, New York, or at Disney World in Orlando, Florida, turkey drumsticks on the grill have been all the rage for years. I remember seeing Disney World visitors walking around with turkey drumsticks in their hands, which always piqued my curiosity. For some reason, though, the turkey leg craze has not taken off up here in the great white north. So, in honour of our neighbours to the south, here is a great turkey drumstick recipe that I may just serve this Canada Day on my annual trip to the Fairmont Kenauk in Montebello, Québec. Either that or I will save it for my traditional July 4th weekend camping trip in Massena, New York.

> 1 1/2 cups (375 mL) beer, *divided*
> 6 cups (1.5 L) water
> 1 medium onion, peeled and sliced
> 4 small turkey drumsticks
>
> 3/4 cups (175 mL) hot sauce
> 1 tsp (5 mL) mustard powder

In large pot or Dutch oven over medium, combine 1 1/4 cups (300 mL) beer, water and onion. Add drumsticks and bring to a boil. Cover and simmer for about 30 minutes.

In small bowl, combine hot sauce, 1/4 cup (60 mL) beer and mustard powder; mix well.

Preheat grill to medium. Place drumsticks on grill and cook for about 30 minutes, basting with hot sauce mixture and turning occasionally, until drumsticks are done and juices run clear.

Grilled Wild Turkey Steaks

(*see* photo p. 124)

Serves 4

The glorious wild turkey is one of Canada's greatest wildlife management success stories. In the 1980s, wild gobblers started to appear in southern and central Ontario and in Québec's Eastern Townships. Since wild turkeys were a resident bird of the United States, it was a real treat to see the odd one around in Canada. Today, thanks to dozens of successful turkey transplant projects across the country and hundreds of volunteer conservationists, the province of Ontario alone now boasts a turkey population of over 100,000 birds. Several provinces have established well-controlled wild turkey hunting seasons for those who wish to pursue them for sport and as table fare. Yes, the glorious gobbler is a prolific and intriguing bird to say the least, and I am always pleased to see them occasionally strutting through my back field.

1/4 cup (60 mL) lemon juice
1/4 cup (60 mL) red-wine vinegar
1/2 cup (125 mL) olive oil
1 Tbsp (15 mL) minced garlic
1/2 tsp (2 mL) salt
1/2 tsp (2 mL) pepper

1 lb (454 g) wild turkey breast, cut into 1-inch (2.5 cm) thick steaks

In large bowl, combine all ingredients except turkey and mix well. Add turkey steaks; stir to cover completely. Cover and marinate in cooler or refrigerator for at least 6 hours.

Prepare campfire, or preheat grill to medium. Remove turkey from marinade. Discard marinade. Grill turkey for about 10 minutes per side until juices run clear. Transfer turkey to serving platter and serve with Campfire Baked Pototoes, p. 80.

Campfire Woodcock

Serves 4

In Canada, game birds are generally categorized as migratory birds or upland game birds. The American woodcock, with its characteristically cylindrical body and long bill, falls into both the migratory bird and upland game bird categories. The woodcock is a terrific table bird with a mildly wild flavour similar to grouse. Once I watched in amazement as a ruffed grouse and an American woodcock walked within inches of each other. Both birds acted like the other one wasn't there. I wish I'd had my camera with me that day!

8 woodcock breasts, cleaned and plucked (*see* Tip)
1/2 cup (125 mL) peanut oil
1 tsp (5 mL) rosemary
1 tsp (5 mL) thyme
1/2 tsp (2 mL) garlic powder
1/2 tsp (2 mL) salt
1/2 tsp (2 mL) pepper

Prepare campfire and establish thick bed of coals. Coat grill with oil or non-stick cooking spray. Rub each woodcock with peanut oil, covering completely. Season each bird with rosemary, thyme, garlic powder, salt and pepper. When grilling surface gets to medium-high (use hand test, p. 5), place woodcock on grid. Cook for about 10 minutes per side until meat is no longer pink. Cook slowly, being careful not to overcook. Serve with Asparagus with Almonds, p. 120.

 tip   **CLEANING AND PLUCKING WOODCOCK**

The American woodcock is a tiny bird and, as with snipe and grouse, the bulk of usable flesh lies in the breast meat. To prepare the woodcock breast for cooking, first remove the wings, legs and head using a sharp kitchen knife or cleaver. Unlike grouse, the woodcock will need to be plucked to expose the breast. Manually pull the feathers out by hand. Don't worry about any small pin feathers remaining, as they will quickly singe and burn off on the grill. Now, tear back the skin on the underside of the bird. Remove and discard the entrails. Then rinse the breast meat under cool water and place on paper towel to dry.

Cheryl's Hearty Chili (p. 35)

Bison Steaks (p. 41)
Grilled Onions (p. 28)
Grilled Tomatoes (p. 134)

Pan-seared Bass over Coals

Serves 4

Bass are an underrated meal fish. Since they tend to be a bit prone to yellow grub, I always take advantage of early season whenever I plan to keep a smallmouth for the table. The smallmouth and largemouth bass fishing season opens usually mid-June, later than almost all other freshwater fish. Bass of the Micropterus family are late spawners and are therefore protected until reproduction is complete. The best bass for eating are those caught in the first week or two of the season, before the lake and river temperatures begin to rise. The flesh of these coldwater bass is generally firm, milky white and delicious.

1/2 cup (125 mL) butter
1/2 tsp (2 mL) vegetable oil
salt and pepper
2 × 2 to 3 lb (900 g to 1.4 kg) bass, cleaned (*see* Tip)
    with head and tail removed
1 large onion, thinly sliced
3 large potatoes, thinly sliced

2 to 3 lemons, sliced

Prepare campfire, or preheat grill to medium, and preheat large skillet. Add butter and vegetable oil. Sprinkle salt and pepper over fish and place in skillet. Add onion and potatoes. Sauté, covered, for about 30 minutes, turning once, until fish flakes easily with a fork and onion and potatoes are soft. Place fish, onion and potatoes on large serving dish. Garnish with lemon slices.

 CLEANING A FISH

To properly clean a fish, start with a good, sharp fillet knife. Begin at the tail and insert the knife into the fish's vent. With a smooth forward stroke, cut through to the centre of the belly to the middle of the gill plate, making sure not to cut too deep. Remove the gills completely, eviscerate the entire fish and discard the organs. Rinse the fish under cold water, and then remove the kidneys (which run along the inside of the backbone) with the end of your thumbnail. Rinse again under cold water and make sure the body cavity is clean and free of debris. Do not remove the head unless the recipe calls for it.

Canadian Fried Bullhead

Serves 6

I am not sure about the rest of the country, but in central Canada, the "bullish" brown bullhead garners a fair amount of attention as a table fish. Since it does require a bit of special preparation compared to most other freshwater fish in Canada, some campers tend to shy away from these whiskered beauties. Once you have mastered the catfish-skinning technique, however, cooking bullheads is a breeze. And as the cliché goes, you cannot judge a book by its cover. The bullhead may not be the most aesthetically pleasing fish, but it is one of the best for eating!

> 2 cups (500 mL) sunflower oil
> 5 to 6 bullheads, skinned (*see* Tip),
>   with head and tail removed
> 1/2 tsp (2 mL) salt
> 1/2 tsp (2 mL) pepper
> 1/4 cup (60 mL) seasoned breadcrumbs
> 1/4 cup (60 mL) flour
> 1 egg, beaten

Prepare campfire, or preheat grill to medium. Heat enough oil in cast-iron skillet to create a shallow fry and cover fish. Test oil temperature with kernel of corn (*see* Tip, p. 91). Season fish with salt and pepper. In shallow dish, combine breadcrumbs and flour. Roll fish in breadcrumb mixture, then dip in the egg. Roll again in breadcrumb mixture. Fry until golden brown on both sides. Place on paper towel–covered serving platter. Serve hot.

 SKINNING CATFISH

Skinning catfish is quite simple once you have done it a couple of times. For this task you need a wood cutting board or fillet table, a pair of pliers, a dry towel and a sharp fillet knife. Start by cutting through the fish's skin just below the head, and cut the skin through 360° around the fish. With a dry towel in your right hand, hold onto the head tightly, and then grab the edge of the fish's skin tightly with the pliers. Pull slowly with your left hand and the skin should peel away much like a sausage casing. Stop when you get to the tail and cut the skin away completely with the fillet knife. Rinse the fish off in cold water and you're all set to go!

Newfie-style Cod Cheeks

Serves 4

You may have heard the legends and rumours surrounding fish cheeks, so I'll set the record straight—everything you have heard is true! The fish's cheeks are the most tender, flavourful and delicious part of the finned creatures. However, smaller fish simply do not produce cheeks worthy of harvesting. Easterners who have enjoyed cod cheeks since the beginning of time know that it is always the larger fish that produce the best cheeks for cooking. The cheeks are a fish's filet mignon, and when it comes to cheeks, size really does matter.

2 Tbsp (30 mL) butter
1 onion, diced
2 garlic cloves, minced
1 tsp (5 mL) salt
1/2 tsp (2 mL) lemon juice
1 tsp (5 mL) dill
1/4 cup (60 mL) white wine

1 lb (454 g) cod cheeks

Prepare campfire, or preheat grill to medium-high. Mix all ingredients except cod cheeks in medium saucepan. Cook until liquid reduces to mushy paste. Reduce heat to medium.

Cut about five 12-inch (30 cm) sections of foil (depending on cheek size) and place 4 to 5 cheeks on each section. Spread sauce thoroughly over cod cheeks and close up foil by folding edges to create small packets. Repeat until all cod cheeks are covered with sauce and packed into small foil packets. Place packets on grill and cook for about 5 minutes on each side until cheeks turn opaque. Serve hot.

 COOKING OIL TEMPERATURE

Cooking with oil can be a fun and tasty way to prepare several outdoor dishes, but finding the right cooking temperature can be difficult without the use of a deep-fry thermometer. A simple technique called the "corn kernel pop" has served me well over the years. You simply drop one popcorn kernel into your oil when it's heating up. The corn kernel will pop open at between 350°F and 375°F (175°C and 190°C), which is the optimal oil temperature for most dishes. Once the kernel has popped, simply take it out and start cooking.

Fried Cod Strips

Serves 4

Although I have enjoyed eating codfish in all of the eastern provinces, my most memorable cod adventure occurred back in 1981 in Seal Cove, Newfoundland. As a boy from central Canada who grew up with mainstream angling techniques, jigging for cod with a hand line from inside a traditional wooden dory was about as primitive a technique as I had ever seen. It did seem strange at first, but it didn't take long to get used to when my first cod hit the gunnels. My father and I had grins from ear to ear as we continued to haul in magnificent codfish hand over fist. As the Newfies would say, that's how you do it, boy!

1/4 cup (60 mL) olive oil
2 lbs (900 g) cod fillet, cut into 1/2-inch (12 mm) strips
pepper
1 1/4 cups (300 mL) coarse breadcrumbs
2 eggs

lemon wedges, for garnish

Prepare campfire, or preheat grill to medium-high. Heat oil in large, steep-sided skillet. Season cod strips with pepper. Spread breadcrumbs on plate. Whisk eggs in medium bowl. Coat cod strips with egg and then coat in breadcrumbs. Place cod strips individually into hot oil. Cook for about 5 minutes, turning once, until golden brown. Transfer fish to paper towel–lined serving platter. Garnish with lemon wedges.

Try with This  Seafood Cocktail Sauce

Makes 2 cups (500 mL)

1/2 onion, minced
2/3 cup (150 mL) horseradish
1 1/2 cups (375 mL) ketchup
1 tsp (5 mL) lemon juice
1 Tbsp (15 mL) cider vinegar
1/2 tsp (2 mL) salt

Blend ingredients together in bowl and mix until smooth. Also try with Bacon Shrimp on the Barbie, p. 118.

Shore Lunch Fried Crappie

Serves 4

A summertime camping or fishing excursion easily turns into a fine meal when panfish are included. The most popular panfish in Canada is the black crappie, found in many of our larger rivers and lakes, and in my opinion it is greatly underutilized. Fishing for crappie can provide the family with hours of enjoyment, and crappies form the foundation for a superb meal back at camp. Given their meagre size, crappie are somewhat labour-intensive to prepare, but you will be rewarded with their big flavour. The best crappies are found in cold, clear waters and are caught early in the season—conveniently, right around the time that camping season begins.

> 1 cup (250 mL) peanut or canola oil
> 1 tsp (5 mL) cayenne pepper
> 1/2 cup (125 mL) mustard
> 10 crappie fillets
> 2 cups (500 mL) corn flour
> salt and pepper, to taste

Prepare campfire, or preheat grill to medium. Heat oil in deep cast-iron skillet. In small bowl, combine cayenne pepper and mustard. Roll up each fillet and use toothpick to hold in place. Brush mustard mixture on each rolled-up fillet. Dip fillets in corn flour. Place fillets in skillet and cook until golden brown. Remove to paper towel to drain; sprinkle with salt and pepper.

Halibut on the Grill

Serves 4

If you have ever seen a halibut, you will understand why this is the largest flatfish in the world. Capable of weighing over 550 pounds (250 kilograms), halibut are highly sought after by sport anglers off the coast of British Columbia. Halibut are famous for their enormous size but also for their taste. Halibut meat is firm, white and very low in fat and oil. If you're looking for a suitable fish to serve while camping or cottaging, halibut makes a great choice as long as you remember that it tends to dry out if cooked too long. Low oil content makes halibut mild and healthy to eat, but also means it has a tendency to stick to the grill, so keep that in mind when cooking halibut on the open fire.

3 Tbsp (45 mL) olive oil
2 cups (500 mL) baby potatoes, quartered
2 cups (500 mL) asparagus, washed well and
   tough ends snapped off
1 onion, sliced
3/4 cup (175 mL) cherry tomatoes

4 × 10 to 12 oz (284 to 341 g) halibut fillets
1/2 tsp (2 mL) salt
1/2 tsp (2 mL) pepper
1/4 cup (60 mL) red-wine vinaigrette dressing

Prepare campfire, or preheat barbecue to medium-high to high. Tear off 4 squares of foil and brush with oil. Divide potatoes, asparagus, onion and tomatoes among foil sheets, placing in centre of sheets. Season fillets with salt and pepper and place on top of vegetables. Drizzle each pile with dressing. Join corners of each foil square to seal tightly. Place packages on grill and cook for about 15 minutes on each side until fish flakes easily when tested with a fork. Open packages carefully and serve hot.

Halibut Brochettes

Serves 4

"You say tomato, I say tomato, let's call the whole thing off." The same tune could be sung for the brochette and skewer as well. In the United States, meat chunks and vegetables cooked on wooden or metal sticks are known as skewers. Here in Canada, the same method is often known as brochettes. Either way you look at it, brochettes or skewers are another cooking technique that simply comes to life when carried out in an outdoor setting. So, call it what you will, brochette or skewer, it's all right to me, just don't call me late for dinner!

> 1/3 cup (75 mL) olive oil
> 1/4 cup (60 mL) white wine vinegar
> 2 Tbsp (30 mL) minced shallots
> 1 Tbsp (15 mL) Dijon mustard
> salt and pepper, to taste
>
> 1 lb (454 g) halibut fillets, cut into 1-inch (2.5 cm) chunks

Mix all ingredients except halibut in small bowl and whisk to blend. Season with salt and pepper. Place fish in glass dish and pour half of marinade over top. Turn to coat; marinate in cooler or refrigerator for 1 hour. Soak wooden skewers in water for 30 minutes (or use metal skewers).

Prepare campfire, or preheat grill to medium-high. Thread fish onto 4 skewers, about 5 to 6 pieces per brochette. Place skewers on grill and cook for 5 to 7 minutes depending on temperature, turning occasionally, until fish chunks are opaque in centre. Serve with Siesta Rice, p. 71, or Grilled Stuffed Peppers, p. 129.

Blackened Perch Fillets

Serves 4

I have often described the taste of perch as walleye on a smaller scale, as perch are a much tinier fish. They are every bit as tasty as walleye and, depending on how you serve them, may just be the best fish meal you've ever had. About 15 years ago, a friend of mine and I spent a great weekend tenting on Little Balsam Lake in Ontario, not far from my hunt camp. At one time the lake was purely trout, but somehow yellow perch made their way in. We decided to take advantage of this accidental introduction by catching as many as we could for dinner. That night we cooked up 18 good-sized perch, or 36 small fillets. It may sound like a lot of fish for two people, but for hungry 20-something-year-old boys, it was just the right amount. That mess of perch proved to me that the spunky green-and-yellow perch rivals all other fish as far as table fare.

1/2 tsp (2 mL) cayenne pepper
1/2 tsp (2 mL) pepper
1/2 tsp (2 mL) thyme
1/2 tsp (2 mL) oregano
1 tsp (5 mL) garlic powder

1 lb (454 g) perch (8 to 10 fillets)
2 Tbsp (30 mL) melted butter

Prepare campfire, or preheat grill to high. Mix cayenne pepper, pepper, thyme, oregano and garlic powder in small bowl. Coat fillets completely in mixture. Coat cast-iron skillet with non-stick cooking spray and preheat on the grill. Place perch in hot skillet and pour melted butter over top. Cook first side until almost charred, then flip over and cook other side until almost charred. Serve piping hot.

Asian Cedar Plank Salmon

(see photo p. 141)

Serves 4

If you have never tried salmon cooked on a cedar plank, then you are missing out on one of the most distinctive-tasting dishes there is. It is believed that cedar plank cooking was introduced by the First Nations of the Pacific Northwest as an alternative to the labour and time-intensive practice of smoking fish. Cedar plank-cooked salmon tastes very much like traditional smoked salmon and boasts the beautiful scent and flavour of the cedar itself. Plank cooking is efficient, too, because the cedar plank itself makes for a good serving platter.

1/3 cup (75 mL) olive oil
1/3 cup (75 mL) soy sauce
1 Tbsp (15 mL) minced ginger
3 tsp (15 mL) minced garlic
1/2 tsp (2 mL) pepper
1/4 cup (60 mL) chopped shallots

4 salmon fillets
1 cedar or applewood cooking plank

In mixing bowl, combine all ingredients except salmon and mix well. Place salmon in shallow baking pan and pour marinade over fish. Marinate salmon for several hours in cooler or refrigerator. Soak plank in water for 1 hour.

Prepare campfire, or preheat grill to medium. Place cedar plank on grill. Remove salmon from marinade and discard marinade. When plank starts to smoke, place fish on plank. Cook for about 20 minutes.

Salmon on the Grill

Serves 4

Most outdoor meals remind me of a location or region in this country that I have visited and spent time camping in. One of my most memorable salmon meals was enjoyed while camping in beautiful White Rock, British Columbia. We were visiting an old friend of the family, Margaret Evermann. Mrs. Evermann was a genuinely warm and outgoing lady of German descent, and she treated us like royalty during our stay. I will never forget the fresh-caught Pacific salmon she served—it has to be some of the best I have ever eaten. Between spending the day in White Rock and enjoying Pacific salmon on the grill with a bit of German flair, it was one heck of a great trip!

> 4 × 6 to 8 oz (170 to 225 g) salmon steaks or fillets
> salt and pepper
> 2 Tbsp (30 mL) olive oil
> 4 lemon wedges

Prepare campfire, or preheat grill to medium-high. Brush grill with oil or coat with non-stick cooking spray. Season salmon with salt and pepper, then brush salmon with oil and place on grill. Cook for 5 to 7 minutes on each side, being careful not to overcook, until fish flakes easily when tested with a fork. Garnish with lemon wedges.

Try with This  ## Lentil Salad

Serves 4 to 6

4 large carrots, diced
1 × 19 oz (540 mL) can drained lentils
1 celery rib, thinly sliced
1/2 red onion, finely diced
2/3 cup (150 mL) Golden Italian dressing
salt and pepper, to taste

In pot over medium, boil carrots until tender. Drain carrots, run under cold water and transfer to large bowl. Add remaining ingredients and mix. Place in cooler or refrigerator for 2 hours before serving.

Sunnies with Marjoram and Lemon Butter

Serves 4

The glorious pumpkinseed, or "sunfish" as it is more commonly called, is a lowly but extremely colourful member of the bass family. Sunnies are generally regarded as a "panfish for kids" and not commonly served as a table fish. Until you have actually tried sunfish, you will never realize how wrong public opinion really is. Granted, the fillets are generally small and their meagre size means they are a bit tricky to clean, but let me tell you, there is nothing wrong with the final product. This marjoram and lemon butter recipe may also be used with bluegill or black crappies.

> **1 cup (250 mL) flour**
> **salt and pepper**
> **4 sunfish, cleaned (*see* Tip, p. 89) and scaled (*see* Tip)**
> **6 Tbsp (90 mL) butter**
> **4 shallots or 3 garlic cloves, chopped**
> **1/2 tsp (2 mL) dried marjoram**
> **1 1/2 Tbsp (25 mL) lemon juice**

Prepare campfire, or preheat grill to medium. Mix flour, salt and pepper in small bowl. Place fish in flour mixture and turn to coat. Melt butter in skillet and add shallots (or garlic), marjoram and sunfish. Cook, covered, for about 5 minutes on each side until browned. Add lemon juice and cook, covered, for about 10 minutes. To serve, pour some lemon butter from pan over each fish.

 SCALING A FISH

For scaling any fish, you require either a fillet knife with a long blade or a metal fish-scaling tool. Begin by placing your fish on a wooden cutting or fillet board. Hold the fish's head down firmly with your left hand and, with the knife in your right hand, begin scraping the fish "against the grain" from tail to head. The scales will loosen and fall off. Continue scraping until the side is smooth and scale-free. Turn the fish over and repeat with the other side. Rinse the fish under cool water to free any lingering scales before cooking.

Campfire Trout and Bacon

Serves 4

The best campfire trout meals are served after a long morning on the water—a true "shore lunch." The idea of the traditional shore lunch is that you cook your catch immediately, right by the lakeshore. To make your shore lunch a success, you will need to pack the right equipment: two large skillets, fresh cooking oil, butter, spices, utensils and all-purpose flour. You can use briquettes or a gas grill; however, the more traditional shore lunch is carried out over open coals. Trust me, after enjoying freshly caught trout cooked up in the great outdoors, you will never want to eat fish at home again.

12 slices bacon
6 brook trout, cleaned (*see* Tip, p. 89) with heads removed
1 cup (250 mL) cornmeal or flour

Fry bacon to desired crispness and transfer to paper towel to drain, reserving bacon fat in skillet. Clean trout thoroughly and wipe dry with paper towel. Roll each trout in cornmeal or flour, making sure to coat evenly. Fry trout in hot bacon fat until it flakes easily when tested with a fork, making sure not to overcook. Serve bacon as a side or save for breakfast.

Campfire Smoked Trout

Serves 6

The first time I had shoreline smoked trout was in northern Québec in 1982. I met a Cree person who was preparing brook trout and lake trout in a makeshift smoker that he had constructed by the lakeshore. We guessed that smoking fish had been this man's tradition for some time because he certainly knew what he was doing. He did not speak English or French, so communicating about the details of his smoker was a bit of a challenge. It seemed that he had been staying at that location for "two moons" and had smoked several species of trout as well as northern pike. The samples he offered us were mouth-wateringly unforgettable.

> 2 cups (500 mL) water
> juice of 1 lemon
> 5 garlic cloves, sliced
> 4 shallots, sliced
> 2 Tbsp (30 mL) salt
> 2 Tbsp (30 mL) sugar
> 2 Tbsp (30 mL) chopped dill
>
> 6 boneless rainbow trout (10 to 12 inches [25 to 30 cm] each)
> lemon juice and horseradish

Mix all ingredients, except trout, lemon juice and horseradish, and mix well. Pour over trout in shallow baking dish. Marinate trout in cooler or refrigerator for 4 to 5 hours if possible (*see* Tip).

Meanwhile, soak some wood chips in water for a few hours. Build a charcoal or briquette fire on one side of your grill and place a shallow pan of water in other half. When coals are hot, scatter wet wood chips on top of coals, which will produce large billows of smoke. Place trout on grill over pan of water, and then put lid or cover over grill to trap smoke inside. Cook for about 30 minutes (depending on amount of smoke). Add lemon juice and horseradish to taste.

 MAKE BEFORE LEAVING

You may want to prepare the marinade and marinate the fish before you arrive in the outdoors. Transport to your outdoor cooking area in a sealed container in a cooler.

Asian Lake Trout

Serves 4

In my opinion, cooking and preparing lake trout Asian-style provides some much-needed flair to one of the blander tasting and less flavourful trout. Don't get me wrong, lake trout is still good, but compared to brook trout, brown trout and rainbow trout, lake trout is neither boldly flavourful nor extremely tasty. It benefits greatly from recipes such as this one. Adding new spices or flavours give this somewhat mundane fish a certain pizzazz.

4 × 6 to 8 oz (170 to 225 g) lake trout fillets

1 Tbsp (15 mL) cornstarch
1/2 cup (125 mL) dark soy sauce
1/4 cup (60 mL) medium dry sherry
2 Tbsp (30 mL) rice vinegar or cider vinegar
2 Tbsp (30 mL) honey

1 cucumber, cut into thin sticks
4 leaves iceberg lettuce
1/4 cup (60 mL) chopped scallions

Rinse and dry trout. Place in ovenproof pan or Dutch oven.

For sauce, mix cornstarch and soy sauce in measuring cup until paste forms. Stir in sherry, vinegar and honey. Pour 3/4 of sauce over trout to coat and let marinate in cooler or refrigerator for 3 to 4 hours. Reserve remaining sauce.

Prepare campfire, or preheat grill to high. Arrange cucumber, lettuce leaves and scallions on 4 plates. Pour remaining sauce into pan and set over barbecue to warm.

Remove trout from marinade, and discard marinade. Cook fish for about 8 minutes per side, brushing frequently with reserved sauce, until firm and opaque. Transfer to plates and pour reserved warmed sauce over them.

Apple Plank Trout

Serves 4

When spending several days in the outdoors, it is of utmost importance that your fish be kept cold and fresh. I have discovered a few refrigeration techniques over the years that don't even require a camping cooler. Dig a hole in the forest floor about 2 feet (60 centimetres) deep and line it with sphagnum moss and ferns. Place your fresh fish in the pit and then cover them with more moss and logs. In most parts of Canada, the early season ground temperatures in May and June remain very cold and provide a natural source of refrigeration for your meat, fish and other food products that need to be kept cool.

1 cedar or applewood cooking plank
2 × 1 1/2 lbs (680 g) trout, cleaned (*see* Tip, p. 89) not filleted
3 Tbsp (45 mL) olive oil

1 tsp (5 mL) salt
1/2 tsp (2 mL) pepper
1 lemon, thinly sliced
1/2 cup (125 mL) chopped fresh dill

Soak plank in water for 1 hour. Prepare campfire, or preheat grill to medium. Lightly coat entire trout with olive oil.

Season inside of fish with salt and pepper and stuff with lemon slices and dill. Place cedar plank on grill. When plank starts to smoke, place fish on plank. Grill for about 15 minutes until fish is opaque and flakes easily. Remove from grill and serve.

Tuna on a Bun

Serves 4

Tuna is one of the most widely used fish species in North America, and for good reason. It is one of the fish highest in omega-3s and provides a great low-fat meal. Keep in mind, though, that if not every camper is a big fan of tuna, you can use salmon or a similar type of fish. With this recipe, you're able to mix and match the fish used to whatever flavour you're interested in at the time. Cooked brook trout, broken into flakes, is a superb Canadian alternative to tuna.

> 1 × 6 oz (170 g) can chunk light tuna, drained
> 1/2 cup (125 mL) breadcrumbs
> 1/3 cup (75 mL) minced onion
> 1/4 cup (60 mL) minced celery
> 1/4 cup (60 mL) minced red pepper
> 1/4 cup (60 mL) mayonnaise
> 1/2 tsp (2 mL) dill
> 1/4 tsp (1 mL) salt
> 1/8 tsp (0.5 mL) pepper
> dash of hot pepper sauce
> 1 egg

In medium bowl, combine all ingredients. Mix well and make 4 patties. Let sit in cooler or refrigerator for 30 minutes to make patties easier to handle.

Prepare campfire, or preheat grill to medium. Grease frying pan or spray with non-stick cooking spray. Cook patties for about 3 to 4 minutes per side until cooked through. Serve on hamburger buns with tomato slices and lettuce leaves and Rice Salad, p. 139.

Mrs. Outdoorsguy's Best-ever Ribs (p. 48)

Outdoor Chicken with Vegetables (p. 59)

Lemon Doré

Serves 4

This recipe is served by many outfitters in Québec and northern Ontario, where the marvellous marble eyes, the walleye, goes by the name *doré*. When guides or chefs at these *pourvoiries*, or lodges, prepare Lemon Doré for their guests, they make it with much pride and effort. Since most Lemon Doré is made from walleye freshly caught that day, you can be sure that it is the freshest meal possible. The ideal-sized fish for this recipe is 2 to 3 pounds (0.9 to 1.4 kilograms): they produce reasonable fillets and represent younger fish specimens, usually 4 years old and younger. The older a walleye gets, the more important it becomes as brood stock for the lake, especially the females. From a conservation standpoint, we should always live-release larger walleyes and retain the smaller ones for eating.

> 4 doré (walleye) fillets
> salt and pepper
> 2 garlic cloves, minced
> 2 lemons, thinly sliced

Prepare campfire, or preheat grill to medium. Lay out four 12 inch (30 cm) pieces of foil. Sprinkle salt, pepper and garlic on fillets and place on foil. Place 2 lemon slices on each fillet. Wrap foil securely around fillets and fold edges to seal. Place fish on grill and cook slowly for about 10 minutes per side until fish flakes easily when tested with a fork.

Plank Walleye

Serves 2

As most Canadians know, the walleye (also known as pickerel or *doré*
depending on where in Canada you live) is perhaps the most popular
freshwater fish for cooking. The sweet, mild flavour of old "marble eyes"
appeals to even non-fish lovers. Often a walleye fishing trip and camping
adventure can be rolled into one. When you are fishing for these prized
freshwater species, keep in mind that you should always keep the skin attached
to your fillets while transporting the fish—it is the law in most provinces.
Doing so allows for identification of the species should you be questioned by
a conservation officer.

> 1 cedar or applewood cooking plank
> 1 tsp (5 mL) dried rosemary
> 1/4 tsp (1 mL) dried parsley
> 1/4 tsp (1 mL) garlic salt
> 1/8 tsp (0.5 mL) salt
>
> 1 Tbsp (15 mL) honey
> 2 Tbsp (30 mL) melted butter
>
> 2 walleye fillets
> 1 tsp (5 mL) olive oil

Soak plank in water for at least 1 hour. In small bowl, combine rosemary,
parsley, garlic salt and salt. In another small bowl, mix honey and melted
butter. Brush walleye fillets with honey and butter mixture and sprinkle
with herb mixture. Place in cooler or refrigerator for 30 minutes to allow
flavours to seep in.

Prepare campfire, or preheat grill to medium. Brush 1 side of plank with
olive oil and place fish in centre. Place plank directly on grill for 20 to
30 minutes until fish flakes easily when tested with a fork. Remove from
grill and serve.

Fried Campfire Walleye

Serves 8

The walleye is perhaps the most sought-after sport fish in all of Canada. Anglers scour our great country each year in search of good lakes that hold this sport fish. Walleye are not necessarily known for their fighting ability, but they are a fish to be reckoned with: anglers pursue them more as a "finesse fish" that requires a certain level of skill to catch. The real bonus of walleye, of course, is the fact that they are simply mouth-watering and may be served in a variety of different ways. Fried Campfire Walleye is one tradition you may want to start this summer—a tradition that will not be difficult to repeat year after year.

3 cups (750 mL) flour, plus extra for dredging fish
3/4 tsp (4 mL) salt
1/2 tsp (2 mL) cayenne pepper
2 × 12 1/2 oz (355 mL) cans of beer,
    preferably Canadian lager or pilsner

peanut (or sunflower) oil, for deep-frying
2 lbs (900 g) walleye fillets (about 12 to 16)

Prepare campfire. Mix flour, salt and cayenne pepper in medium bowl. Whisk in beer until consistency is smooth.

Pour peanut oil into large cast-iron skillet and heat over hot coals. Pat walleye fillets dry with paper towel. Cover in flour, shaking off excess. Dip each fillet individually into beer batter and place gently in hot oil. Deep-fry until golden brown, turning only once. Use a slotted spoon (not a fork!) to transfer fish to paper towel–lined baking sheet or plate.

Asian Whitefish Brochettes

Makes 12 brochettes

Wild Canadian whitefish are the perfect choice for any camping trip. They are solid white, boast a beautiful, mild flavour and have a great history. Did you know that whitefish were once the most important commercial fish in Canada? They are found mostly in cold northern lakes and often are associated with lake trout, which have a similar habitat. Lake whitefish are often caught on lake bottoms by ice fishermen during winter. Whitefish are ideal for a variety of outdoor dishes and are also great on the smoker!

1 1/2 lbs (680 g) boneless whitefish fillets
1 cup (250 mL) canned pineapple pieces in liquid
1 large red pepper

1 Tbsp (15 mL) soy sauce
2 Tbsp (30 mL) brown sugar
2 Tbsp (30 mL) white vinegar
2 Tbsp (30 mL) ketchup
1/2 tsp (2 mL) salt

Soak wooden skewers in water for 30 minutes (or use metal skewers). Cut whitefish into 1-inch (2.5 cm) cubes. Drain pineapple pieces, reserving 2 Tbsp (30 mL) liquid. Slice red pepper into 1-inch (2.5 cm) pieces. Thread red pepper, fish and pineapple alternately onto skewers.

Lay whitefish brochettes in shallow dish. Add reserved pineapple juice to soy sauce, and mix in brown sugar, vinegar, ketchup and salt in small bowl. Pour marinade over brochettes. Cover and let stand in cooler or refrigerator for 2 to 3 hours.

Prepare campfire at least 1 hour in advance until you have 3 inches (7.5 cm) of hot coals. Remove brochettes from marinade, and reserve marinade. Grill brochettes, brushing frequently with marinade. Cook on each side until just cooked through. Serve with Rice Salad, p. 139.

Whitefish on the Grill

Serves 6

Of all the white-filleted freshwater fish in Canada, whitefish boast some of the most pleasant flavours. They are typically found in deep, coldwater lakes of the Canadian Shield and are harvested extensively by First Nations communities. Whitefish are mild, flavourful and moist with a low oil content, and they can be used in a variety of recipes. Whitefish live a long time and grow very slowly in cold northern waters, which may have something to do with their crisp, clean taste.

2 lbs (900 g) whitefish fillets
2 green peppers, sliced
2 onions, sliced

1/4 cup (60 mL) melted butter
2 Tbsp (30 mL) lemon juice
2 tsp (10 mL) salt
1 tsp (5 mL) paprika
1/2 tsp (2 mL) pepper

Prepare campfire. Cut fish into serving-sized portions. Cut six 12 × 12 inch (30 × 30 cm) squares of foil and grease lightly. Place 1 portion of fish, skin-side down, on each piece of foil and top with green pepper and onion.

Mix remaining ingredients in small bowl and pour over fish. Fold foil packages so they are sealed and place on grill about 5 inches (12.5 cm) from moderately hot coals. Cook for 45 to 60 minutes until fish flakes easily when tested with a fork.

Grilled Lobster

Serves 8

Lobster can be a rather costly food and many people consider it somewhat of a delicacy, but that is no reason not to enjoy it outdoors. Mild, flavourful grilled lobster will be a hit with the whole family. What we do in our family to divide the lobster equitably is to separate the cooked meat into claw meat and body meat. Depending on the pickiness of your eaters, some will only eat the more tender flesh of the lobster claws, while others (like myself) who thoroughly enjoy all parts of the lobster usually end up with the slightly less tender body meat. Because hard-shell Canadian lobster can be tricky to open, leave that job to an experienced "shell cracker"—a less experienced person could actually sustain a serious injury.

1 cup (250 mL) butter
2 Tbsp (30 mL) chopped chives

4 × 1 1/2 lbs (680 g) uncooked lobsters
salt and pepper
2 lemons, quartered

Prepare campfire, or preheat grill to medium. Melt butter in small saucepan and add chives; set aside. Split each lobster: remove intestines, stomach and gills from body cavity, leaving only empty shell. Remove claws where they attach to body. Break claws with claw cracker or hammer and remove meat. Place meat in shells.

Place open lobster cut-side up on grill. Cook for 15 to 20 minutes, basting with chive butter frequently, until meat is opaque. Place lobsters on large platter and season with salt and pepper. Serve with lemon quarters.

Pan-seared Mussels

Serves 2

I have visited many regions of Canada over the years, and I often feel like I've camped in almost every provincial park in the country. One region in particular I remember seeing firsthand is the beautiful Malpeque Bay in Prince Edward Island—home of the world-famous Island Blue mussels. Staring out over the red sand of the bay, I remember wondering what it was that made this part of Eastern Canada so special as to be the birthplace for the most famous mussels known to man. It is a breathtakingly beautiful setting, and maybe that's what makes the difference, I thought. Was it the water or perhaps the skilled commercial mussel farmers that make it so special? Perhaps some things are just better when not overanalyzed.

> 2 lbs (900 g) mussels, cleaned and de-bearded (*see* Tip)
> 2 Tbsp (30 mL) olive oil
> 1 Tbsp (15 mL) crushed garlic
> 2 Tbsp (30 mL) chopped chives
>
> salt and pepper

Prepare campfire, or preheat grill to high. Heat dry cast-iron pan or skillet for 10 minutes. Drop mussels into pan and steam for about 5 minutes until they open. Meanwhile, mix olive oil, garlic and chives in bowl.

After mussels have steamed open, discard any that did not open after 1 minute. Pour oil mixture over mussels and season with salt and pepper. Serve immediately.

 tip   DE-BEARDING MUSSELS

Mussels have a group of fibres known as a "beard" that can be seen protruding through the shell. The beard needs to be removed before eating. The best way to complete this task is by using a dry towel to grasp the threads. Give them a good tug toward the hinge-end of the mussel. If you pull the beard out toward the opening end of the mussel by mistake, you may actually tear the mussel on the inside of the shell, which will kill it instantly. An improperly extracted beard may spell the end of your mussel.

Barbecued Oysters

Serves 4

Each fall during hunting season, the boys and I indulge in decadent seafood feasts. One year it was a huge feed of home-prepared calamari; another time it was king crab legs, as well as shrimp and seafood bisque. One very memorable meal was when I served fresh oysters and explained the proper techniques for shucking and eating to those who had never tried them. I will never forget the sight of all those wonderful oysters spread out over the camp's kitchen table, which we had covered in newspaper. I don't recall how many oysters we ate that evening, but it was easily several dozen. For me, enjoying seafood means sharing it with close friends in the most beautiful setting I can think of, a rustic old camp built by my grandfather in the scenic Laurentian Mountains of Québec.

20 fresh oysters in the shell
2 cups (500 mL) Seafood Cocktail Sauce (*see* p. 92)
1 lemon
salt and pepper

Preheat barbecue to medium-high. Arrange oysters on grill in 1 layer; avoid overlapping. Cook oysters for 10 to 12 minutes until they begin to open. Discard any oysters that do not open after 15 minutes. Remove from grill. Once cooled slightly, open each oyster, remove top shell and spread out on large serving platter. Spoon a dab of seafood cocktail sauce on top of each oyster. Squeeze some lemon juice over top and sprinkle lightly with salt and pepper. Serve immediately.

Grilled Scallops

Serves 6

The lovely little sea scallop is like the tenderloin of the sea. If you hail from a town like Digby, Nova Scotia—Canada's Scallop Capital—scallops are more than just seafood; they are a way of life. And if you have never tried scallops on the grill, or served any other way for that matter, you are missing out on a little slice of heaven. I would describe the taste as slightly sweet and not unlike Atlantic lobster or crab. Scallops have a unique consistency when cooked properly and a mild, buttery smooth flavour that appeals to even the non-seafood lover. But keep an eye on your scallops when you're preparing them on the grill because they tend to overcook very easily.

> 3/4 cup (175 mL) butter
> 2/3 cup (150 mL) chopped onion
> 3 garlic cloves, chopped
> 1/4 cup (60 mL) lemon juice
> 1/2 tsp (2 mL) salt
> 2 lbs (900 g) scallops

Prepare campfire, or preheat grill to medium; lightly oil cooking surface. Melt butter in saucepan. Add onion and garlic and cook until soft. Remove saucepan from heat. Stir in lemon juice and salt. Put scallops in bowl and pour butter mixture over top. Let stand for about 5 minutes.

Place scallops in fine-mesh barbecue grill or grill basket. Cook for about 5 minutes until opaque. Meanwhile, put butter mixture back on heat and bring to a boil. Lower heat until scallops are cooked. Transfer scallops to serving platter; pour butter mixture over top and serve.

Barbecued Cajun Shrimp

Serves 4

Our environment is of the utmost importance, so I always try to achieve what I refer to as "low-impact camping." Basically, it means enjoying our great outdoors without causing any negative impact. You can achieve low-impact camping at your site by trying not to damage or make any drastic changes to the landscape. Don't cut down every tree in sight or dig large drainage ditches, and make sure your garbage is picked up before you leave. It always gives me a good feeling to know I have left a camp area the same at the end of the trip as it was when I arrived. It's also a joy to return to your favourite spot the following year and find it in the same condition you left it.

> 2 garlic cloves, minced
> 1/3 cup (75 mL) Worcestershire sauce
> 3 Tbsp (45 mL) tomato-based barbecue sauce
> 1 Tbsp (15 mL) minced onion
> 1 Tbsp (15 mL) pepper
> 1 tsp (5 mL) salt
> 1/4 tsp (1 mL) hot pepper sauce, or more to taste
>
> 1 1/2 lbs (680 g) medium-large to large shrimp, peeled and de-veined (*see* Tip, p. 117)
> 3 Tbsp (45 mL) butter, cut into chunks
> 2 Tbsp (30 mL) lemon juice

Mix all ingredients, except shrimp, butter and lemon juice, in large bowl. Slowly stir in shrimp. Let shrimp sit in mixture for 30 minutes at room temperature.

Prepare campfire and establish coals to high (use hand test, p. 5). Drain marinade from shrimp and pour it into medium saucepan. Bring marinade to a rolling boil for several minutes. Add butter, stirring until completely melted. Remove from heat and stir in lemon juice. Set aside.

Place several layers of foil, large enough to hold shrimp in one layer, over cooking surface. Poke holes in foil every few inches to allow air and moisture in. Spray foil with non-stick cooking spray. Cook shrimp on foil on grill for 2 to 3 minutes per side, basting often with sauce, until no longer shiny or translucent.

Grilled Shrimp with Salsa

(*see* photo p. 142)

Serves 4

When cooking shrimp, prawns, scallops or any other type of seafood on the grill or over an open fire, remember that they all cook very quickly. Your seafood is done when it turns from a shiny translucent exterior to a solid, pearly opaque colour. Try to keep your prawns and shrimp away from the open flame and avoid extremely hot fires; your seafood dish will turn out much better for it.

> 1 × 14 oz (398 mL) can stewed tomatoes
> 1 orange, peeled and chopped
> 1/4 cup (60 mL) sliced green onion
> 1/4 cup (60 mL) chopped cilantro or parsley
> 1 Tbsp (15 mL) olive oil
> 1 to 2 tsp (5 to 10 mL) minced jalapeño pepper
> 1 small garlic clove, crushed
> salt and pepper, to taste
>
> 1 lb (454 g) medium shrimp, peeled and de-veined (*see* Tip)

Prepare campfire, or preheat grill to medium-low. Soak wooden skewers in water for 30 minutes (or use metal skewers).

To make salsa, drain tomatoes, reserving liquid. Chop tomatoes and combine with reserved liquid, orange, green onion, cilantro, olive oil, jalapeño pepper and garlic in mixing bowl. Season with salt and pepper. Set aside.

Thread shrimp on skewers; season with salt and pepper if desired. Brush grill with oil. Cook shrimp until they turn just opaque pink. Top with salsa and serve over Vegetarian Rice, p. 76.

 PEELING AND DE-VEINING SHRIMP

Use your thumbs to peel back the sides of the shrimp shell. Slowly pull away any fibres of legs that remain once the shell has been removed. Hold the body of the shrimp and gently tug on the tail. The shell will come off with the tail. To de-vein shrimp, use a small, sharp knife to make a shallow cut down the back, exposing the vein. Pull the vein out gently with your fingers.

Bacon Shrimp on the Barbie

Serves 6

Although shrimp are typically quite simple to cook in an outdoor setting, they are also one of the easiest foods to overcook, and nowhere is this more true than on an outdoor grill. Always keep a close eye on the colour and texture of your shrimp; shrimp can change from perfectly cooked to overcooked in a matter of seconds. You can recognize that your shrimp is done by its opaque colour and firm texture. Leaving shrimp on the grill for even an extra minute or two past the point of proper cooking will mean tough and chewy shrimp.

1/2 cup (125 mL) olive oil
1/2 tsp (2 mL) sugar
1 small onion, finely chopped
1/2 tsp (2 mL) garlic powder
1/4 tsp (1 mL) salt
1/2 tsp (2 mL) pepper

1 lb (454 g) shrimp, peeled and de-veined (*see* Tip, p. 117)
1/2 lb (225 g) bacon slices, cut in half lengthwise and crosswise

To make marinade, combine oil, sugar, onion, garlic powder, salt and pepper in small bowl. Place shrimp in bowl or container. Pour marinade over shrimp and place in cooler or refrigerator for at least 4 hours.

Prepare campfire, or preheat grill to medium-low. Partially cook bacon in frying pan. Remove from pan and drain well in paper towel. Wrap 1 piece of bacon around each shrimp, securing with wooden toothpick. Arrange 5 wrapped shrimp together on pieces of foil. Fold foil tightly. Grill shrimp in foil until shrimp are opaque and bacon is cooked. Serve with Seafood Cocktail Sauce, p. 92.

Canadian Tea Biscuits

Serves 6

3 cups (750 mL) self-rising flour
1/2 tsp (2 mL) sugar
4 Tbsp (60 mL) butter

3/4 cup (175 mL) milk
1 egg

1/2 cup (125 mL) all-purpose flour

Preheat oven to 400°F (205°C) and grease 2 baking sheets. Mix self-rising flour and sugar in large bowl. Cut butter into small chunks and add to bowl. Mix well. In separate bowl, whisk milk and egg together. Add to flour mixture and stir until batter becomes doughy.

Sprinkle all-purpose flour on hard surface and spread out. Knead dough until smooth. Flatten into rough rectangle with your hands or rolling pin. Cut into biscuits with knife or cookie cutter. Place biscuits on baking sheets and bake for about 10 minutes until golden brown.

Garlic Couscous

Serves 4

1 Tbsp (15 mL) extra-virgin olive oil
1 garlic clove, minced
1 cup (250 mL) couscous
1 cups (250 mL) chicken broth
1/3 cup (75 mL) grated fresh Parmesan cheese
salt and pepper

Prepare campfire, or preheat grill to medium-high. Heat oil and garlic in medium saucepan until oil bubbles slightly. Add couscous and chicken broth. Bring to a boil and simmer for 3 minutes. Add Parmesan cheese, salt and pepper, and serve.

Campfire Mac and Cheese

Serves 4

Granted, it may not be fancy, but my daughter Grace and I love eating Campfire Mac and Cheese! We simply can't get enough of it, and we have no problem going on about it all the way through the meal. We often prepare two different meals on the night when Campfire Mac and Cheese is being served because no one else seems to appreciate it quite the same way we do.

    4 cups (1 L) water
    1 tsp (5 mL) salt
    4 cups (1 L) elbow macaroni, uncooked
    2 Tbsp (30 mL) butter
    1 cup (250 mL) milk
    1 cup (250 mL) shredded medium Cheddar cheese

Prepare campfire, or preheat grill to medium. Combine water and salt in medium pot and bring to a boil. Add macaroni and boil, stirring often, until *al dente* (firm but not crunchy). Drain macaroni carefully. Add butter, milk and cheese, mixing until creamy. Best served with ketchup on the side as a dip.

Asparagus with Almonds

(*see* photo p. 124)

Serves 4

    2 lbs (900 g) fresh asparagus, washed well and tough
      ends snapped off

    1/4 cup (60 mL) butter
    1/4 cup (60 mL) slivered almonds
    1 Tbsp (15 mL) lemon juice
    1/2 tsp (2 mL) salt
    1/2 tsp (2 mL) pepper

Prepare campfire, or preheat grill to medium. Boil asparagus in pot of water or steam in vegetable steamer until tender and bright green.

In cast-iron skillet, melt butter and cook almonds until browned. Add lemon juice and heat for 2 minutes until sauce thickens. Add salt and pepper and stir. Pour over cooked asparagus and serve. This side dish is great served with Grilled Pheasant, p. 81, or Campfire Woodcock, p. 86.

Sides and Salads

Beets with a Bite

Serves 6 to 8

2 Tbsp (30 mL) butter
1 Tbsp (15 mL) flour
2 Tbsp (30 mL) brown sugar
3 Tbsp (45 mL) white vinegar
1/4 cup (60 mL) boiling water
1/2 tsp (2 mL) salt
1/4 tsp (1 mL) paprika
1/4 tsp (1 mL) ground cinnamon
4 cups (1 L) sliced, cooked beets

Preheat oven to 350°F (175°C). Melt butter in saucepan over medium to high. Add flour and sugar; whisk until smooth. Add vinegar, water, salt, paprika and cinnamon and mix well. Stir constantly until mixture is bubbling. Place beets in greased casserole dish. Pour mixture over top. Cover and bake for about 30 minutes.

Cheesy Brussels Sprouts

Serves 4

24 Brussels sprouts, washed and trimmed
3 Tbsp (45 mL) olive oil, *divided*
1/4 tsp (1 mL) salt
1/4 tsp (1 mL) pepper
1/4 cup (60 mL) grated Cheddar cheese

Prepare campfire, or preheat grill to medium. Cut sprouts in half and place in bowl. Add 2 Tbsp (30 mL) olive oil and toss gently. In large skillet, heat remaining olive oil. Place sprouts flat-side down in skillet. Season with salt and pepper and cook, covered, until Brussels sprouts are cooked and brown on flat side. Remove cover and shake skillet so sprouts toss around and brown on round side. Once lightly browned, sprinkle with salt, pepper and cheese. Remove from skillet. Serve and enjoy.

Corn on the Grill

Serves 4

The first time I ever tried corn on the grill, I was blown away by how good it tasted! My friends and I were camping along the shores of Lake Ontario just outside of Kingston, and we spent the weekend fishing and enjoying the warm summer air. This corn was one of the meals we had—and one of the best camping meals I have ever had. The grill was at an ideal temperature and the corn on the cob came off as a thing of beauty. Never discount corn as a tasty meal you can serve the whole family in a natural outdoor setting. As John Steinbeck wrote in *Of Mice and Men*, it is somewhat like "living off the fat of the land," which sounds pretty darn terrific to me.

8 ears corn, husks removed
1 Tbsp (15 mL) canola oil
1/4 lb (113 g) butter, cut in a solid block
salt and pepper, to taste

Prepare campfire, or preheat grill to medium-high (use hand test, p. 5). Coat corn with oil and grill for 15 to 20 minutes, flipping occasionally, until golden brown and sugars in corn are caramelized. Allow corn to cool slightly and serve rolled in butter. Add salt and pepper.

Quesadillas on the Grill (p. 66)

Grilled Wild Turkey Steaks (p. 85)
Asparagus with Almonds (p. 120)

Grilled Vegetarian Eggplant

Serves 4

According to the latest statistics, 4 percent of all Canadians are proclaimed vegetarians (compared to 2.8 percent of all Americans), which means that eventually you may be cottaging or camping with a friend or relative who does not eat meat. Recipes such as this one are perfect to add to your bag of outdoor tricks for these types of occasions. During our traditional Labour Day get-togethers, the Morrison family is mindful of those of us who do not consume a lot of meat. My sister Karen is "close to being vegetarian," so we always keep a couple of vegetable dishes at the ready.

2 large eggplants, cut into 1-inch (2.5 cm) slices
1/3 cup (75 mL) extra-virgin olive oil
1/2 tsp (2 mL) salt
1/2 tsp (2 mL) pepper

1 loaf thick-sliced Italian bread
1 cup (250 mL) fresh mozzarella cheese
1 lb (454 g) sliced tomatoes
3 Tbsp (45 mL) balsamic vinegar

Prepare campfire until good layer of coals is formed. Brush eggplant slices with olive oil and season with salt and pepper. Place eggplant on hot grill over fire. Cook slices until brown on bottom, then flip over. Brush other side with olive oil and cook until brown. Remove from heat.

Grill bread slices with same technique, brushing each side with oil and cooking until lightly browned. Arrange toasted bread on platter with cheese, eggplant and tomato slices. Drizzle with balsamic vinegar.

Campfire Eggplant

Serves 4

In Canada, we are used to seeing eggplants that are purple in colour and oval in shape, but have you ever seen an eggplant that is white, yellow, rose, black, green or striped? Different varieties may be difficult to find locally, but they are available in specialty vegetable markets across Canada.

1 eggplant, cut into 1/2-inch (12 mm) slices
1/2 tsp (2 mL) salt
1/4 cup (60 mL) extra-virgin olive oil
2 tsp (10 mL) balsamic vinegar
1/2 tsp (2 mL) dried oregano
pinch of salt
pinch of pepper

Prepare campfire, or preheat grill to medium. Sprinkle eggplant with salt and let stand for 10 to 15 minutes to allow moisture to seep out. Pat dry with paper towel. In mixing bowl, combine olive oil, balsamic vinegar, oregano, salt and pepper. Mix well and brush half of mixture over eggplant. Place eggplant slices on grill. Cook, covered, for about 10 minutes until tender, turning once and brushing with remaining oil mixture.

Baked Onions

Serves 4

4 large onions, peeled
1/4 cup (60 mL) butter, cut into pieces
1 tsp (5 mL) salt
1/4 tsp (1 mL) pepper
1 cup (250 mL) shredded Parmesan cheese

Prepare campfire, or preheat grill to medium, or preheat oven to 400°F (205°C). Cut each onion into 8 pieces. Tear off and grease 4 squares of foil and place 8 onion pieces on each square. Put a couple of pieces of butter on top of each onion. Sprinkle with salt, pepper and cheese. Wrap foil around onions to form little packets. Throw packets on grill or bake on baking sheet in oven for about 1 hour.

Québec Sautéed Têtes de Violon

Serves 4

When I was growing up, picking fiddleheads was a big Morrison family tradition. My parents would pack up my sisters and me in the old Pontiac Biscayne, and we would head off for a day of "plucking heads." We quickly learned how to cut and bag the curly natural food and that the "furry-looking ones" were not good for eating. As I recall, it was great fun; the only downside was that, since my mother only ever served them steamed, I did not really enjoy the taste all that much. Over the years I discovered more decadent ways to cook these immature ferns, and sautéed is certainly one of my favourites. If only I had discovered this delicious recipe many years ago!

1/4 cup (60 mL) butter
1/2 cup (125 mL) finely minced onion
1 Tbsp (15 mL) minced garlic
3 Tbsp (45 mL) thinly sliced wild garlic (optional)
1 lb (454 g) têtes de violon (fiddleheads), rinsed
1/2 tsp (2 mL) salt
1/2 tsp (2 mL) pepper
1 Tbsp (15 mL) lemon juice
1 Tbsp (15 mL) sugar

Prepare campfire. Heat butter in cast-iron skillet over hot coals and fry onion, garlic and wild garlic (if desired). Cook until garlic and onion have softened. Add fiddleheads to skillet and stir. Add salt, pepper, lemon juice and sugar, and sauté until fiddleheads are tender.

Stuffed Onions

Serves 4

6 large Spanish onions
2 cups (500 mL) dry bread cubes
2/3 cup (150 mL) chicken broth
1/4 lb (113 g) fresh Italian sausage,
    cut into 1/4-inch (6 mm) slices

Prepare campfire, or preheat grill to medium-low. Leave skin on onions and trim off both ends of each onion to make flat bottoms. Keep onion tops to put back later. Hollow out centre of each onion, leaving 2 or 3 outer layers intact. In medium bowl, soak bread cubes in chicken broth. When broth is completely absorbed, add sausage. Mix gently.

Stuff onions with sausage mixture. Place tops back on onions. Place each onion upright in centre of piece of heavy-duty foil; bring up edges and seal, leaving a little space for expansion of steam.

Cook each packet upright until tender. Remove onions from foil, remove outermost onion skin and serve.

Buttery Snow Peas

Serves 4

2 cups (500 mL) fresh snow peas, ends removed
1 Tbsp (15 mL) butter
1 Tbsp (15 mL) chopped shallots
salt and pepper

Boil peas in pot of water for 5 minutes until tender. Drain and place back in pot. Add butter and warm until butter melts, stirring peas to cover. Top with shallots, salt and pepper, and serve.

Grilled Stuffed Peppers

Serves 4

I will never forget my mother serving large trays of stuffed peppers at the Maplewood Inn, the hotel my parents owned for 25 years and where I grew up. I can still picture the kitchen ladies pulling them out of the oven and how delicious they smelled. The aroma was almost intoxicating! As a result, Grilled Stuffed Peppers remain one of the meals I serve today on our trips to the Ottawa Valley. Isn't it amazing how a certain dish can bring back so many fond memories? For me, this dish harkens back to a simpler time.

4 red peppers
1 × 10 oz (284 mL) can corn
1/2 cup (125 mL) breadcrumbs
1 egg, beaten
1 Tbsp (15 mL) flour
2 Tbsp (30 mL) diced onion
2 Tbsp (30 mL) chopped parsley
2/3 cup (150 mL) Golden Italian dressing

Prepare campfire, or preheat grill to medium-high. Cut three 3/4 to 1 inch (2 to 2.5 cm) rings from each pepper and spread out on lightly oiled foil. Combine corn, breadcrumbs, egg, flour, onion, parsley and dressing in bowl. Spread mixture into pepper rings and pack tightly.

Fold foil around pepper rings into pyramid shape. Pinch edges together to seal packet. Place packet over coals or briquettes for about 15 minutes until mixture is golden brown and peppers have softened. Let peppers cool for 5 minutes before serving.

Potato Skewers

Serves 4

When we think of potatoes in Canada, we automatically think of Prince Edward Island, the hub of potato production. But did you know that other provinces such as Manitoba, New Brunswick and Alberta also boast substantial potato crops each year? Of all the potatoes grown in Canada, over half are processed into French fries. Prince Edward Island accounts for about one-quarter of the country's potato industry, although Manitoba is a close second with over 20 percent of the market. In my opinion, Prince Edward Island potatoes are still the tastiest, perhaps owing to the rich red soil and ideal growing conditions.

8 small red potatoes (about 1 lb [454 g])
2 Tbsp (30 mL) chopped fresh basil
1 Tbsp (15 mL) vegetable oil
1/2 tsp (2 mL) salt
1/2 tsp (2 mL) pepper

Soak wooden skewers in water for 30 minutes (or use metal skewers).

Prepare campfire, or preheat grill to medium. Wash potatoes and cut in half. In pot, parboil potatoes in salted water for about 10 minutes to tenderize. Remove potatoes from water and sprinkle with basil, oil, salt and pepper.

Thread potatoes onto skewers. Place on grill and cook, covered, for about 10 minutes, turning occasionally, until desired doneness.

Foiled Potatoes and Onions

Serves 4

The great thing about Foiled Potatoes and Onions is that you can cook it either over the open coals or on top of a cooking grid. A cooking grid or grill surface is the preferred method because the potatoes and onions do cook a bit slower on the grid than they would sitting directly on top of the coals, which helps to prevent burning. I usually look for 4 baseball-sized rocks on which to position my cooking grid. I find 2 to 3 inches (5 to 7.5 cm) from the coals to be the perfect distance.

> **4 medium potatoes**
> **1 onion**
> **3 Tbsp (45 mL) butter**
> **Montréal steak spice**
> **sour cream (optional)**

Prepare campfire, or preheat grill to high. Cut potatoes into slices about 1/4-inch (6 mm) thick but only about 3/4 through each potato; the potatoes will be held together at the bottom. Cut onion into thinner slices. Place onion slices in between potato slices and top with small pieces of butter. Sprinkle Montréal steak spice on top and wrap potatoes in heavy-duty foil to form little packets. Cook for about 30 minutes, turning occasionally. Unwrap foil, serve and enjoy. Top with sour cream if you desire.

Campfire Skillet Potatoes

Serves 6

> **2 to 3 lbs (900 g to 1.4 kg) potatoes, unpeeled**
> **2 Tbsp (30 mL) canola oil**
> **1/2 tsp (2 mL) salt**
> **1/2 tsp (2 mL) pepper**

Prepare campfire. Place potatoes in cast-iron pan and add enough water to cover. Bring to a boil. Once water has boiled off, check tenderness of potatoes. If potatoes have not reached desired tenderness, leave in skillet above coals until skins are crispy. Drizzle with canola oil and season with salt and pepper.

Garlic Mashed Potatoes

Serves 4

1 Tbsp (15 mL) butter
3 garlic cloves, chopped
3 bulbs wild garlic, finely chopped (optional)
2 lbs (900 g) potatoes, peeled and halved
1/2 cup (125 mL) buttermilk
1/2 tsp (2 mL) salt
1/4 tsp (1 mL) pepper

Prepare campfire, or preheat grill to medium. Melt butter in small skillet and fry garlic and wild garlic (if desired) until cooked. Meanwhile, in medium saucepan, boil potatoes in salted water until tender. Drain potatoes and return to pot. Add cooked garlic, buttermilk, salt and pepper. Mash with hand mixer or potato masher until potatoes are light and fluffy.

Butternut Squash

Serves 4 to 6

1 ripe butternut squash
1/3 cup (75 mL) butter
1 Tbsp (15 mL) brown sugar

Cut squash into 4 or 6 pieces and remove seeds. Place in vegetable steamer in pot with water in bottom. Cover and steam for about 30 minutes until squash can be easily pierced with a fork. Let cool. Spoon out squash into cooking pot, leaving skin behind. Mash squash with potato masher. Add butter and brown sugar and reheat.

Sweet Potato Packets

Serves 1

Not only are sweet potatoes a great alternative to regular potatoes, but they have also been voted by nutritionists at the Centre for Science in the Public Interest (CSPI) as the number one vegetable from a health standpoint. A total of 18 different vegetables were compared as to their respective amounts of beneficial components such as complex carbohydrates, dietary fibre and vitamins A and C. The comparison also looked at such things as fat content, cholesterol, sodium and caffeine. The sweet potato outranked its competition by nearly two to one in all areas, making it a superb choice for all nutrition-conscious outdoor enthusiasts.

1 sweet potato, peeled and cut into wedges
1/2 small fennel bulb, sliced
3 tsp (15 mL) orange juice, *divided*
3 tsp (15 mL) olive oil, *divided*
grated orange peel
2 tsp (10 mL) red-wine vinegar
1 tsp (5 mL) honey
1 Tbsp (15 mL) chopped flat-leaf parsley
1 Tbsp (15 mL) chopped walnuts
1/4 cup (60 mL) crumbled feta cheese

Prepare campfire, or preheat grill to medium. Tear off 12 × 12 inch (30 × 30 cm) square of heavy-duty foil. Place potato and fennel in centre of foil and spoon 1 tsp (5 mL) orange juice and 1 tsp (5 mL) olive oil over top. Wrap foil square so it is sealed, allowing a bit of room for expansion. Place packet on grill for 35 to 45 minutes until potatoes are soft.

In small bowl, combine 2 tsp (10 mL) orange juice, 2 tsp (10 mL) olive oil, orange peel, vinegar, honey, parsley and walnuts. Remove packet from grill and carefully open. Pour mixture over cooked potatoes and sprinkle with feta cheese. Place packet back on grill for a few minutes to heat, or serve immediately.

Grilled Tomatoes

(see photo p. 88)

Serves 4

4 firm, ripe tomatoes
1/4 cup (60 mL) extra-virgin olive oil
salt and pepper, to taste
4 basil leaves, thinly sliced

Prepare campfire, or preheat grill to high. Cut tomatoes in half and remove seeds and pulp. Lightly brush olive oil on cut side of tomatoes and sprinkle with salt and pepper. Place tomatoes on grill, cut-side down. Cover and cook for 2 to 4 minutes.

Remove tomatoes from grill and place cut-side up on serving plate. Drizzle a little more olive oil on tomatoes and sprinkle with basil and salt and pepper.

Mother Nature's Grilled Veggies

(see photo p. 52)

Serves 4 to 6

1 cup (250 mL) thinly sliced white mushrooms
1 red pepper, cut into strips
1 small zucchini, cut into 1/4-inch (6 mm) slices
3 Tbsp (45 mL) melted butter
1 Tbsp (15 mL) crushed fresh thyme
1 Tbsp (15 mL) chopped fresh chives
1 garlic clove, minced
1/4 tsp (1 mL) salt
1/4 tsp (1 mL) pepper

Prepare campfire, or preheat grill to medium. Combine mushrooms, red pepper and zucchini in medium bowl. Combine butter, thyme, chives, garlic, salt and pepper in small bowl. Pour mixture over vegetables and toss to coat.

Tear off 1 × 2 ft (30 × 60 cm) sheet of foil and place vegetables on it. Wrap securely and place packet on grill for about 25 minutes until vegetables have reached desired tenderness. Open packet carefully and serve.

Skewered Vegetables

Serves 4

Cooler space can become an issue while camping, so vegetable dishes like this one are perfect because the vegetables do not necessarily require refrigeration. A meal or a side dish of Skewered Vegetables will make your life a lot easier. I like to pick up the vegetables for this dish at one of the local farmers' vegetable stands by the side of the road. Nothing beats the taste of ripe, locally grown fruits and vegetables, and it is nice to support local farmers.

1 large onion
1 green pepper
1 red pepper
8 medium white mushrooms
8 cherry or grape tomatoes

1/2 cup (125 mL) olive oil
1 garlic clove, minced
1/4 tsp (1 mL) salt
1/4 tsp (1 mL) pepper

Cut onion, green pepper, red pepper, mushrooms and tomatoes into similar-sized pieces. In large bowl, combine oil, garlic, salt and pepper. Toss vegetables in marinade and place in cooler or refrigerator for 3 hours.

Prepare campfire, or preheat grill to medium. Soak wooden skewers in water for 30 minutes (or use metal skewers). Thread vegetables onto skewers and sprinkle with salt to taste. Cook for 10 to 15 minutes, rotating regularly, until vegetables have reached desired tenderness.

Grilled Zucchini Fries

Serves 6

1 cup (250 mL) breadcrumbs
5 Tbsp (75 mL) grated Parmesan cheese
2/3 cup (150 mL) Golden Italian dressing
3 medium zucchini, cut into French fry–sized strips
1/2 tsp (2 mL) salt
white vinegar and ketchup to serve

Prepare campfire and place greased cooking grid 3 to 4 inches (7.5 to 10 cm) from coals. Combine breadcrumbs and Parmesan cheese in mixing bowl. Place dressing in another bowl. Dip zucchini strips first in dressing and then roll in breadcrumbs. Spread out zucchini fries on grid and cook, turning often, until crisp and light brown in colour. Sprinkle with salt and serve with white vinegar and ketchup.

Green Bean Salad with Almonds

Serves 6

1 lb (454 g) fresh green beans
1 × 10 oz (284 mL) can mandarin orange segments, drained
1/4 cup (60 mL) raspberry vinaigrette dressing
3 Tbsp (45 mL) sliced almonds

Steam or boil beans until tender. Drain beans and rinse under cold water to cool. Cut beans into 1- to 2-inch (2.5 to 5 cm) pieces. Place in serving bowl and add remaining ingredients; mix well and serve.

Classic Caesar Salad

Serves 6

1/4 cup (60 mL) olive oil
7 Tbsp (105 mL) grated Parmesan cheese, *divided*
1 Tbsp (15 mL) white-wine vinegar
2 tsp (10 mL) Dijon mustard
3 garlic cloves, minced
1/2 tsp (2 mL) salt
1/2 tsp (2 mL) pepper
3 Tbsp (45 mL) mayonnaise

6 pre-washed Romaine hearts
2 1/2 cups (625 mL) croutons

Whisk all ingredients, except lettuce, croutons and 4 Tbsp (60 mL) Parmesan, in bowl until smooth.

Cut romaine hearts lengthwise into 1-inch (2.5 cm) strips. Place in extra-large salad bowl. Add dressing, croutons and remaining Parmesan cheese and toss to combine.

Carrot Salad

Serves 4

2 cups (500 mL) grated carrots
1 Tbsp (15 mL) apple cider vinegar
1 Tbsp (15 mL) olive oil
1 Tbsp (15 mL) lemon juice

Place carrots in medium bowl. Add vinegar, olive oil and lemon juice. Mix well and serve.

Summer Potato Salad

Serves 6

10 large potatoes, peeled
6 hard-boiled eggs, shelled and chopped
2 celery ribs, chopped
1 medium onion, finely chopped
2 cups (500 mL) mayonnaise
2 Tbsp (30 mL) sweet pickle relish
1/2 tsp (2 mL) salt
1/2 tsp (2 mL) pepper

Prepare campfire, or preheat grill to medium. In large pot, boil potatoes in salted water until tender. Drain potatoes and cool by running cold water over them. Cube potatoes and place in large bowl. Add eggs, celery and onion.

In separate bowl, combine mayonnaise, relish, salt and pepper and mix well. Add to potatoes and mix well. Cover and let stand in cooler or refrigerator for a few hours before serving.

Macaroni Salad

Serves 4

2 cups (500 mL) water
2 cups (500 mL) uncooked elbow macaroni
1/2 cup (125 mL) mayonnaise
2 hard-boiled eggs, shelled and chopped
1/4 cup (60 mL) chopped celery
1/3 cup (75 mL) chopped shallots
2 tsp (10 mL) sugar
2 tsp (10 mL) vinegar
1/2 tsp (2 mL) prepared mustard
salt and pepper, to taste

Prepare campfire, or preheat grill to medium. Boil water in medium pot. Add macaroni and cook until *al dente* (firm but not crunchy). Drain macaroni and rinse with cold water to cool completely. Return macaroni to pot. Add remaining ingredients and stir well. Place in cooler or refrigerator for 2 hours before serving.

Golden Italian Chef's Salad

Serves 4

6 cups (1.5 L) iceberg lettuce, cut into bite-sized pieces
6 slices ham, cut into strips
4 hard-boiled eggs, shelled and sliced
3 tomatoes, cut into wedges
3 bulbs wild garlic, sliced (optional)
2 Tbsp (30 mL) bacon bits
1 cup (250 mL) shredded Cheddar cheese
1 cup (250 mL) Golden Italian dressing

Divide lettuce among 4 salad plates. Top each plate of lettuce with ham, egg, tomato, garlic and bacon. Sprinkle cheese on top and drizzle with dressing.

Rice Salad

Serves 4 to 6

2 cups (500 mL) water
1/2 tsp (2 mL) salt
1 Tbsp (15 mL) butter (or olive oil)
1 cup (250 mL) uncooked long grain white rice
1 cup (250 mL) green peas
1/4 cup (60 mL) chopped green pepper
1/4 cup (60 mL) chopped celery
1 Tbsp (15 mL) finely chopped shallots
1 Tbsp (15 mL) vegetable oil
1/4 tsp (1 mL) ground nutmeg
1/2 tsp (2 mL) salt
1/2 tsp (2 mL) pepper

In medium saucepan over high, add water, salt and butter and bring to a boil. Add rice and stir. Reduce heat to medium-low, and simmer, covered, for 15 minutes. Turn off heat, fluff rice with a fork and keep covered for 5 minutes.

Combine cooked rice, peas, green pepper, celery and shallots in large bowl. Mix remaining ingredients together in separate bowl. Pour into rice bowl and mix. Cover and place in cooler or refrigerator for 2 hours before serving.

Red-wine Vinegar Marinade

Makes 1/3 cup (75 mL)

3 Tbsp (45 mL) red-wine vinegar
3 Tbsp (45 mL) olive oil
2 tsp (10 mL) minced garlic
2 tsp (10 mL) oregano
1/2 tsp (2 mL) salt
1/2 tsp (2 mL) pepper

Place all ingredients in bowl and mix well. Use as marinade for chicken, lamb, pork or beef.

Thai Marinade

Makes 1 cup (250 mL)

1/2 cup (125 mL) brown steak sauce
1/3 cup (75 mL) creamy peanut butter
2 Tbsp (30 mL) soy sauce

Combine ingredients in small bowl. Mix well and let stand in cooler or refrigerator for 1 hour before using. A great marinade for chicken, pork or beef.

Pork and Beef Marinade

Makes 1 cup (250 mL)

5 garlic cloves, chopped
2 Tbsp (30 mL) Worcestershire sauce
2 Tbsp (30 mL) balsamic vinegar
2 tsp (10 mL) Dijon mustard
1/3 cup (75 mL) vegetable oil
1/2 tsp (2 mL) pepper

Combine all ingredients in bowl and mix well. This marinade is great for steak or pork tenderloin.

Asian Cedar Plank Salmon (p. 97)

Grilled Shrimp with Salsa (p. 117)

Veggie Marinade

Makes 1 cup (250 mL)

2/3 cup (150 mL) olive oil
1/3 cup (75 mL) balsamic vinegar
1/4 cup (60 mL) minced onion
1 Tbsp (15 mL) chopped fresh basil
1 tsp (5 mL) minced garlic
1/2 tsp (2 mL) salt
1/4 tsp (1 mL) pepper

Combine all ingredients in bowl and mix well. This marinade is great for grilled vegetables, but don't marinate vegetables in it for more than 3 or 4 hours or they will get soggy.

Chicken Spicy Dry Rub

Makes enough for 1 large chicken

1 tsp (5 mL) salt
1 tsp (5 mL) cayenne pepper
2 tsp (10 mL) paprika
2 tsp (10 mL) pepper
2 tsp (10 mL) chili flakes
4 tsp (20 mL) brown sugar

Mix all ingredients in bowl. Rub all over chicken; grill chicken on campfire grid or on barbecue rotisserie.

Family Salsa

Makes 2 cups (500 mL)

3 Tbsp (45 mL) finely chopped onion
2 small garlic cloves, minced
2 cups (500 mL) boiling water
3 large ripe tomatoes, peeled and seeds removed, chopped
2 jalapeño peppers, finely chopped
1/2 tsp (2 mL) salt
1/2 tsp (2 mL) pepper

Place onion and garlic in strainer and pour boiling water over top. Allow to drain thoroughly and let cool. Combine with tomatoes, jalapeño peppers, salt and pepper. Let stand in cooler or refrigerator for at least 1 hour before serving.

Avocado Salsa

Makes 1 cup (250 mL)

2 plum tomatoes, chopped
1 ripe avocado, peeled, pitted and chopped
1/4 cup (60 mL) finely chopped red onion
1 garlic clove, minced
1 Tbsp (15 mL) chopped fresh oregano
1 Tbsp (15 mL) olive oil
1 Tbsp (15 mL) white-wine vinegar

In mixing bowl, combine all ingredients and stir. Cover and let stand in cooler or refrigerator for 2 hours before serving. Makes a great snack with plain tortilla chips.

Down-home Horseradish

Makes 1 cup (250 mL)

1 cup (250 mL) peeled, cubed horseradish root
3/4 cup (175 mL) vinegar
2 tsp (10 mL) sugar
1/4 tsp (1 mL) salt

Place all ingredients in food processor or use hand mixer to blend until puréed. Transfer to bowl and let stand in cooler or refrigerator for 1 hour before serving. Goes well with shrimp and red meat, or a dash will give some added snap to a Bloody Caesar.

Tzatziki Sauce

Makes 2 cups (500 mL)

3 Tbsp (45 mL) olive oil
1 Tbsp (15 mL) white vinegar
2 garlic cloves, minced
1/4 tsp (1 mL) pepper
1 cup (250 mL) strained Greek-style yogurt
1 cup (250 mL) sour cream
1 tsp (5 mL) chopped dill
1/2 tsp (2 mL) salt

In medium bowl, combine all ingredients and mix well. Let stand in cooler or refrigerator for at least 2 hours before serving. A great condiment for sandwich wraps and burgers.

Cranberry Relish

Makes 3 cups (750 mL)

2 Granny Smith apples
1 large, whole seedless orange
2 cups (500 mL) raw cranberries
1 1/2 cups (375 mL) sugar
  (or less or more, depending on desired sweetness)

Core and cut apples and place in food processor or grinder. Leave peel on orange and cut into sections. Add orange sections and cranberries to food processor. Chop fruit into 1/3-inch (1 cm) cubes, then transfer to medium bowl. Add sugar and mix well. Let sit for 1 hour before serving.

Cheese Sauce

Makes 1 1/2 cups (375 mL)

2 Tbsp (30 mL) butter
2 Tbsp (30 mL) flour
1 cup (250 mL) milk
3 processed cheese slices

Prepare campfire, or preheat grill to medium. Melt butter in saucepan. Add flour and mix to form paste. Slowly add milk, a little at a time, and whisk continuously. Once sauce has thickened, add cheese slices and whisk until cheese has melted and sauce is smooth. Great on all vegetables, especially broccoli, cauliflower and asparagus.

Italian Salad Dressing

Makes 2 cups (500 mL)

2 Tbsp (30 mL) dried oregano
2 Tbsp (30 mL) salt
1 Tbsp (15 mL) dried parsley
1 Tbsp (15 mL) onion powder
1 tsp (5 mL) dried basil
1 tsp (5 mL) pepper
1/4 tsp (1 mL) dried thyme
1/4 tsp (1 mL) celery salt
1/4 cup (60 mL) white vinegar
2/3 cup (150 mL) olive oil

Combine dry ingredients in small sealable plastic bag or small container with lid. Seal or cover, and shake to mix. To make dressing, mix 2 Tbsp (30 mL) of dry mixture with vinegar and olive oil. You can store container of dry ingredients and make salad dressing whenever you want it.

Coleslaw Dressing

Makes 1 1/2 cups (375 mL)

1 cup (250 mL) mayonnaise
1/2 cup (125 mL) sugar
1 Tbsp (15 mL) white vinegar
1/2 Tbsp (7 mL) horseradish
1/4 tsp (1 mL) celery seed

Combine all ingredients in bowl and mix well. Cover and place in cooler or refrigerator. Use as dressing for your favourite coleslaw recipe.

Campfire Scrambled Eggs

Serves 4

When scrambled eggs are served in a wrap, the already great taste of eggs—combined with cheese and red peppers—becomes a delicious, convenient finger food the whole family can enjoy. The great thing about cooking scrambled eggs over the open fire in the morning is that you will often have enough hot coals left over from the night before. If that is the case, place your skillet right on top of the coals and cover it while frying the peppers. With some luck, the fire will be hot enough that the eggs are cooked in a few short minutes.

1 Tbsp (15 mL) vegetable oil
1 red pepper, chopped
6 eggs
2 Tbsp (30 mL) milk
1/4 tsp (1 mL) salt
1/4 tsp (1 mL) pepper
1 cup (250 mL) Cheddar cheese, shredded
4 large tortillas

Prepare campfire, or preheat grill to medium. In large skillet, heat oil and fry red pepper until softened. Mix eggs, milk, salt and pepper together and pour into pan. Cook until eggs are light and fluffy.

Sprinkle cheese down centre of each tortilla and spoon egg mixture over cheese. Fold top and bottom of tortilla over filling, and fold in sides to form rectangle. Lightly heat in pan and turn until tortillas are crisp and golden.

Breakfasts

Western Scrambled Eggs

Serves 6

3 Tbsp (45 mL) butter
12 eggs
3 slices cooked ham, cut into cubes
salt and pepper, to taste

Heat butter in large frying pan or skillet over medium-low. In medium bowl, beat eggs together. Add ham, salt and pepper. Pour mixture into frying pan and cook, scraping bottom of pan and mixing eggs. When eggs are fully cooked, remove from pan and enjoy. Eggs can also be placed on toast to make western sandwiches for lunch.

Hard-boiled Eggs on the Campfire

Make as many as you like

I have mixed feelings about hard-boiled eggs and camping. Hard-boiled eggs have typically been our last meal before breaking down camp each spring while fishing in the Abitibi–Témiscamingue region, which is always sad. They are, however, an easy, wholesome breakfast food as well as a great filler for sandwiches. So when you are making eggs this way, throw on a few extras and you can make egg salad for sandwiches later. You can satisfy most morning appetites with a hard-boiled egg, and eggs are high in protein and easy to prepare. Keep in mind that the newspaper needs to be damp throughout, otherwise it'll catch fire and scorch the eggs!

1 egg in shell
newspaper

Dampen newspaper and wrap egg in it. Bury newspaper-wrapped egg in coals and wait 5 to 8 minutes, depending on how well you like your egg cooked. Take package out of coals, and unwrap and shell egg. It will come out just like a hard-boiled egg!

Egg and Bean Breakfast Burrito

Serves 4

For some people, beans and camping have evolved into somewhat of a love-hate relationship. Just ask Grant Bailey of Ottawa. While preparing dinner one evening in the wilds of eastern Ontario, Grant's dad hauled out a can of beans from a dwindling food pack and placed it smack dab in the middle of the campfire. Grant was concerned about this, but his father assured him that if the can was placed with the seam pointing up, it would heat through and separate along the weakest point, the seam. As dinner preparations progressed, Grant glanced in hungry anticipation at the hefty can of warming beans. All of sudden, a loud kapoff echoed through the hills! There were hot beans everywhere: on the tent, on the ground, in the trees, and covering Grant and his father. Once the initial shock had passed, father and son laughed uncontrollably. After dutifully recovering what beans they could, a lesson was learned and a new dish—known as "beans and bark"—was created.

> 1 × 14 oz (398 mL) can black beans
> 1 cup (250 mL) salsa (*see* Family Salsa, p. 144)
> 4 eggs
> 1/4 cup (60 mL) milk
> 4 flour tortillas
> 1/2 cup (125 mL) shredded Cheddar cheese

Prepare campfire, or preheat grill to medium. Place black beans in pot. Add salsa and bring mixture to a boil; remove from heat and set aside.

Preheat frying pan over medium. Crack eggs into medium bowl. Add milk and whisk. Pour egg mixture into frying pan and cook as you would scrambled eggs.

When eggs are done, make each burrito. Lay tortillas out flat. Layer with eggs and a scoop of bean and salsa mixture. Top with cheese. Fold up tortillas and serve.

Morning Baggy Omelettes
Serves 1

The first time I tried Morning Baggy Omelettes, I must admit I was a tad skeptical. They almost seemed too easy to be true—and as it turned out, I was correct. My big mistake the first time was using a small sealable sandwich bag. Evidently, it was not thick enough to handle such heat—it shrivelled up like a raisin and actually melted into the eggs. I didn't give up and discovered by asking around that the recipe will indeed work well if you use heavy-duty, freezer-style sealable bags instead. So I tried again with the thicker bags, and what do you know, they worked like a charm!

> 1 large heavy-duty, freezer-style sealable bag
> 2 eggs
> 2 Tbsp (30 mL) milk
> additions such as cheese, diced ham, mushrooms or
>   cooked bacon pieces

Have pot of boiling water ready over campfire or camp stove. Crack eggs into sealable bag and add milk and whatever additions you desire. Seal bag well and slosh ingredients around.

Throw bag into boiling water and allow to boil for about 3 minutes. Remove bag with tongs. Empty contents onto plate, and presto, you have a beautiful omelette (it flips over like an omelet right in the bag while cooking).

Hearty Top-of-the-Morning Casserole

Serves 4

Of all the meals you can prepare outdoors, there is just something magical about that first meal of the day. It may have something to do with the fact that I am a real morning person, but getting a jump on the day is really important to me. As the fire gets crackling, I can see the fog lifting off the lake and hear the distant call of our Canadian loon. Getting breakfast started before anyone is awake is a secret passion of mine, but I don't often admit that because people would think I'm nuts. Whether it's traditional eggs and bacon or this Hearty Top-of-the-Morning Casserole, there is nothing more enjoyable than preparing breakfast with the cool morning air in your lungs. And there is no better way to build a strong appetite!

> **6 eggs**
> **1 small onion, chopped**
> **1 small red pepper, chopped**
> **1 package frozen shredded hash browns**
> **sausage (cooked and diced) or chopped ham**
> **1 cup (250 mL) grated mild Cheddar cheese,** *divided*

Prepare campfire, or preheat grill to medium. In small bowl, beat eggs well, and add chopped onion and red pepper.

Spray skillet with non-stick spray, or grease it well. Place hash browns on bottom of skillet. Place sausage or ham on top of hash browns. Pour egg and vegetable mixture over meat. Top with 1/2 cup (125 mL) cheese and cook, covered, for 5 minutes until egg has begun to be omelette consistency. Turn once and sprinkle 1/2 cup (125 mL) cheese on top. Cook, covered, for about 5 minutes until cheese is melted.

152 Breakfasts

Hunt Camp Breakfast Quiche

Serves 6

As with most hunt camps that I know, each member of my camp plays a certain role around camp so that chores get done and things run as smoothly as possible. After the woodstove has been stoked, my first job of the day is preparing breakfast for six hungry men. That task can be enough to handle at the best of times, but since breakfast preparation usually begins around 3:30 AM, I need to be on the ball to keep things under control. Most days, I serve the boys a traditional Canadian hunters' breakfast of thick-sliced bacon, sausage, pan-fries made with onions and potatoes from the night before and, of course, eggs. This fall, however, I plan to make things easier on myself with a hearty Hunt Camp Breakfast Quiche.

1/2 lb (225 g) bacon, sliced into small pieces
1 medium onion, diced
1/2 lb (225 g) ground pork sausage
12 eggs
1 × 2 lb (900 g) bag frozen diced hash browns
1/2 lb (225 g) shredded Cheddar cheese

Prepare campfire, or preheat grill to medium, and preheat Dutch oven. Brown bacon and onion in Dutch oven; drain bacon fat. Add ground sausage and hash browns and cook for 15 minutes until potatoes begin to brown. Meanwhile, beat eggs together in bowl. Pour over bacon mixture and cook for 10 to 15 minutes until eggs have started to set. Add cheese over eggs. Cook until eggs are set completely and cheese has melted. Slice and serve.

Wild Blueberry Maple Pancakes

(see photo p. 159)

Serves 4 to 6

Anyone who lives in the Canadian Shield has surely picked wild blueberries from time to time. There are so many productive wild blueberry regions in Canada, and so many recipes, including this one, that you can use this wonderful berry in. Some of my most memorable wild blueberry picking took place near Peterborough in central Ontario. On my trips back to college in Lindsay at the end of the summer, I would regularly park the old Volare along the side of Highway 7 so I could pick a basketful of wild blueberries. The bog country along that stretch of highway was the perfect habitat for blueberries, and I wasn't about to miss out.

> 4 Tbsp (60 mL) pure Québec maple syrup, *divided,*
>   plus more for serving
> 2 cups (500 mL) wild blueberries, *divided*
> 1 cup (250 mL) flour
> 1 tsp (5 mL) baking powder
> 1/2 tsp (2 mL) baking soda
> 1 cup (250 mL) milk
> 1 egg, beaten
> 2 Tbsp (30 mL) melted butter

In small pot, heat 2 Tbsp (30 mL) maple syrup until just warm. Add 1 cup (250 mL) blueberries to syrup and mash. Heat syrup and blueberries until mixture just starts to boil. Remove from heat and set aside.

In bowl, combine flour, baking powder and baking soda and mix well. In separate bowl, combine milk, egg, butter, 2 Tbsp (30 mL) maple syrup and 1 cup (250 mL) blueberries. Pour wet batter into dry ingredients and mix well.

Preheat grill to medium. In pan or greased skillet, pour about 1/4 cup (60 mL) batter (*see* Tip). When deep holes or bubbles appear in pancake, flip over and cook other side. Repeat for each pancake. Serve with blueberry syrup.

 *tip*   PANCAKE SIZE

Pancakes flip easily when they are made to match the size of your flipper.

Waffle-maker Waffles

Serves 4

Admittedly, using a waffle-maker over the open campfire is not the fastest method of making waffles, but speed really is beside the point. The real joy of preparing outdoor treats like homemade waffles in a traditional waffle-maker is making them yourself on a campfire you built with your own two hands. Little tasks such as this make spending time in the fresh air so rewarding. Sure, it is much simpler to drop a couple of frozen waffles into the toaster at home, but trust me, the taste and satisfaction of cooking them over the fire will far exceed any fun you have with a waffle at home.

1 cup (250 mL) flour
1 Tbsp (15 mL) sugar
1/2 tsp (2 mL) salt
1 egg
1 cup (250 mL) sour cream
1/2 cup (125 mL) milk
1 tsp (5 mL) baking powder
1/4 tsp (1 mL) baking soda
3 Tbsp (45 mL) melted butter or margarine

Grease and preheat waffle iron over hot coals. In large mixing bowl, combine all ingredients and mix well. Pour 1/2 cup (125 mL) mixture on waffle iron. Close waffle iron and cook for about 5 minutes on each side until waffle is light golden in colour. Serve with real Québec or Canadian maple syrup.

Traditional French Toast

Serves 4

When you are looking for something a little different than bacon and eggs for breakfast, French toast is always a great alternative. I have yet to meet anyone who does not enjoy French toast in the great outdoors. Perhaps it is the sweetness of traditional French toast when topped with natural maple syrup that gets people going, or it could be the buttery fried flavour of the bread as it comes off the pan. French toast is a real hit in my outings and will surely be a success in your outdoor adventures as well.

> butter
> 4 eggs
> 1 cup (250 mL) milk
> 1/2 tsp (2 mL) ground cinnamon
> 8 slices bread
> powdered sugar (optional)

Prepare campfire, or preheat grill to medium-low. Preheat frying pan or skillet and melt a bit of butter in pan or spray with non-stick cooking spray. Meanwhile, combine eggs and milk in small bowl. Add cinnamon and beat with a fork. Dip bread slices into egg mixture and place in heated pan. Cook each side for about 2 to 3 minutes until bread is nicely browned. Remove from pan and sprinkle with powdered sugar if desired. Serve with your favourite syrup or topping.

 SAVOURY FRENCH TOAST

For a variation of French toast, use salt and pepper instead of cinnamon and ketchup instead of powdered sugar.

Solar Oven Zucchini Bread

Makes 1 loaf

Cooking a dessert like zucchini bread in the solar oven will put your solar culinary skills to the ultimate test! Always use a black baking pan. I use an older loaf pan that has honestly seen better days, but it is ideal for the solar oven. Since it is nearly impossible to burn anything in a solar oven, it is important to know the approximate internal temperature of your oven for the length of time you leave the loaf to cook. Keep an eye on your zucchini bread and begin using the toothpick test after about 2 hours, though depending on the conditions, it may take much longer than that.

3 eggs
2 tsp (10 mL) vanilla extract
1 cup (250 mL) vegetable oil
2 cups (500 mL) grated zucchini
2 cups (500 mL) sugar
3 cups (750 mL) white flour
1/4 tsp (1 mL) baking powder
3 tsp (15 mL) ground cinnamon
1 tsp (5 mL) baking soda

Combine eggs, vanilla extract, vegetable oil, zucchini and sugar in bowl and mix well. Add remaining ingredients to mixture and stir. Place mixture in dark pan and cook in solar oven for 2 to 3 hours (or more) until a toothpick inserted into bread comes out clean.

Dutch Oven Coffee Cake

Makes 1 cake

Putting together a well-thought out dessert such as this cake, along with a main course and suitable side dish, will take planning and a fair amount of work in an outdoor setting. On weekend-only trips, I try to leave the more extravagant meals with desserts for Saturday night when there is more time for preparation. When you arrive at the cottage or campsite on Friday, try to think of something simpler and less labour-intensive. For me, Dutch Oven Coffee Cake is a Saturday night dessert, and trust me, it is well worth the wait.

> 1 × 18 1/4 oz (517 g) box golden cake mix
> 2 ripe bananas
> 1 tsp (5 mL) melted butter
> 1/2 tsp (2 mL) ground cinnamon
> 1 tsp (5 mL) flour
> 3/4 cup (175 mL) brown sugar

Prepare campfire, or preheat grill to medium. Place a few small stones or balls of foil in bottom of Dutch oven. Put pie tin on top of stones. Prepare cake mix according to package directions and pour batter into pie tin. Mash bananas and pour into pie tin.

Combine butter, cinnamon, flour and brown sugar in small bowl and mix. Sprinkle on top of bananas in pie tin. Cover Dutch oven and cook for about 30 minutes until a toothpick inserted into cake comes out clean.

Wild Blueberry Maple Pancakes (p. 154)

S'mores (p. 163)

Campfire Cinnamon Buns

Serves 4

I have learned to face the fact that camping is not the time to go on a diet. There is just something about sleeping in tents or in a rustic camp that brings out a healthy appetite in people. One tends to be more active when spending time outdoors as well, so enjoying a hearty meal just seems to fit right in. Besides, it would be no fun at all to count calories during a camping trip— there are so many more enjoyable things you could be doing with your time!

1 × 8 oz (226 g) tube refrigerator biscuits
3 Tbsp (45 mL) melted butter
1/4 cup (60 mL) sugar
2 tsp (10 mL) ground cinnamon

Prepare campfire. Unwrap package of refrigerator biscuits and stretch them around roasting sticks. Cook over open fire until browned. Brush on melted butter. Combine sugar and cinnamon. Spread cinnamon mixture out on plate and then roll biscuit in it.

Orange Shell Muffins on the Campfire

Make as many as you like

As ridiculous as this recipe sounds, Orange Shell Muffins on the Campfire are fun and easy to prepare, and they provide great snacks on camping trips. The kids will enjoy helping make these muffins as well as eating them later. This recipe is one of my children's favourites; for my girls, the fire can't produce coals quickly enough to get these muffins going.

packaged dry muffin mix (add-water-only type works well)
oranges

Prepare campfire. Prepare muffin mix according to package directions. Cut slice off top of each orange and scoop out flesh. Set flesh aside to eat later. Fill orange shells with prepared muffin mix. Put orange tops back on and wrap in foil. Bake directly on hot coals for about 30 to 40 minutes. When muffins are done, scoop them out and eat them.

Best-ever Pie Iron Pie
Serves 1

There's no reason to put your pie iron away after dinner, because you can use it to prepare several desserts. Did you know that in the Australian outback, these gadgets are known as "jaffle irons" and are used to cook a variety of traditional Aussie meals? Residents of Africa also use a campfire toaster similar to a jaffle iron, and in the United States, the popular Toastwich was a portable toasted sandwich maker dating back to the 1920s. My preferred pie iron brand, the Cuisor, is made in France, but it is really no different than the other pie irons of the world.

2 slices bread
2 or 3 Tbsp (30 or 45 mL) cherry, blueberry,
   strawberry or apple pie filling

Prepare campfire. Butter 1 side of each slice of bread. Place 1 slice of bread (butter-side down) on 1 side of iron. Spread your favourite pie filling on bread. Top with second slice of bread (butter-side up). Close iron and trim any excess bread so it does not catch fire. Heat over hot coals until hot and bread is lightly toasted.

Baked Apple over the Open Fire
Serves 1

On any given weekend during the summer, there will be a virtual cornucopia of great summertime snacks like this one at the Morrison campfire. The crazy thing is how impressed our guests always are. I just haven't the heart to tell them just how easy many of these campfire recipes are. My guess is that most people are simply too intimidated to try new things, but I say, why not? But be prepared to bring a well-stocked cooler with you: the news of your cooking endeavours will undoubtedly spread like wildfire.

1 apple
raisins
brown sugar
ground cinnamon

Prepare campfire. Core apple and place on square of foil. Fill hole with raisins, brown sugar and dash of cinnamon. Wrap with foil and bake for 10 minutes on hot coals. Unwrap and enjoy—but be careful, it's hot!

S'mores

(*see* photo p. 160)

Serves 1

S'mores are to camping what claws are to lobster, or what whiskers are to catfish. Basically, you can't have one without the other, especially if there are young people around camp. The earliest known reference to this standard campfire treat was by the Girl Scouts organization in a publication dating back to 1927. And since both my daughters are Girl Guide members, I have asked them to pass along my thanks at their next meeting. The next time you enjoy a s'more, you should thank a Girl Scout—or Girl Guide—for it!

**1 marshmallow
chocolate chips (or flat chocolate bar pieces)
2 graham crackers**

Prepare campfire. On green stick or roasting stick over coals, cook marshmallow until golden brown. Put on top of graham cracker, top with chocolate chips and complete by topping with another graham cracker. Yum yum!

Peanut Butter S'mores

Serves 1

This past summer we decided to experiment a little because I felt the traditional s'mores recipe was getting to be a bit overused. It was as simple as replacing the chocolate chips or chocolate bar chunks with a peanut butter cup. I can't believe I never thought of it sooner, but Peanut Butter S'mores are the bee's knees when it comes to campfire treats. I suggest you throw a few packages of peanut butter cups in with your camping supplies this summer!

**1 marshmallow
1 peanut butter cup
2 graham crackers**

Prepare campfire. On green stick or roasting stick over coals, cook marshmallow until golden brown. Put on top of graham cracker, top with peanut butter cup and complete by topping with another graham cracker.

Apple Pie on a Stick

Make as many as you like

When Aerie Biafore of Orleans, Ontario, was 13 years old, his mother sent him on a weeklong canoe camping trip to Algonquin Provincial Park. After three days of pitching tents and collecting firewood in the pouring rain, Aerie was soaking wet, tired and ready to go home. But one morning when he awoke, the sun was shining overhead and the camp leaders were cooking bread over the fire. Everyone was given a clump of dough to mould over the end of a stick. It was the neatest thing he had ever seen. They filled the dough with peanut butter, jelly or apple pieces and cooked it until it was golden brown. As he bit into the bread he had cooked himself, Aerie remembers thinking that he could do anything he put his mind to. The sweet campfire treat was a real turning point for the distraught 13-year-old, and something he never forgot.

red or green apple
ground cinnamon
sugar

Prepare campfire until good layer of coals is formed. Push green stick or roasting stick through 1 apple and turn stick over campfire coals, roasting apple as you would a marshmallow. When apple peel starts to loosen, carefully peel off (adults, you will have to help children peel apple). In bowl, mix cinnamon and sugar. Roll your apple in mixture until evenly coated on all sides. Roast over fire for a few more minutes and let cool before eating.

Campfire Banana Split

Makes 1

1 banana
brown sugar
chocolate bar, chopped (or chocolate chips)
mini marshmallows

Slice banana carefully down middle, but leave it in peel. In slit, sprinkle brown sugar, chopped chocolate bar and mini marshmallows. Wrap in foil and heat 3 to 4 inches (7.5 to 10 cm) from hot coals for about 10 minutes. Let stand briefly before opening.

Summer Camp Apple Sauce

Serves 4

Cooking outdoors during the summertime presents certain risks and hazards. Open fires, regardless of how small or large they are, pose a potential risk of forest fire, and you owe it to yourself to be familiar with the Canadian Fire Weather Index (FWI). It is a tool created by Natural Resources Canada for rating the degree of forest fire danger across the country 24/7. Based on factors such as moisture content and relative humidity in different regions of the country at any given time, the FWI gives a sense of how dangerous an open fire might be. Fire risk is plotted from low and moderate risk to high and extremely high risk of forest fire. When the risk of forest fire is the highest, there will be an outright ban on campfires, so always check whether there are any fire bans before you decide to cook these apples or anything else over the campfire this summer.

4 apples
3/4 cup (175 mL) water
1/4 cup (60 mL) sugar
1/2 tsp (2 mL) ground cinnamon

Prepare campfire. Peel and core apples and cut into chunks. Place in medium skillet and mix in remaining ingredients. Cover and cook about 4 inches (10 cm) above coals until apples have softened. Remove from heat and cool. Mash with potato masher and serve in small bowls.

Caribbean Bananas

Makes 1

I've enjoyed several memorable trips to Jamaica with my wife, and these roasted Caribbean Bananas are an island tradition that I just had to try at home. When I first saw this recipe being prepared in Jamaica, I was told it was "Irie." I was not quite sure what that meant at the time, but after several trips to that island paradise and several roasted bananas later, I came to understand the meaning of Irie.

**1 banana
sugar
juice of 1 lemon**

Put ripe, unpeeled banana into ashes of a good fire. Roast for about 30 minutes until skin looks black. Remove banana from ashes very carefully and split down centre. Sprinkle banana inside with sugar and lemon juice. Eat as you like, with a spoon or your fingers.

Pineapple Treat

Serves 6

Have you ever crunched into a piece of pineapple and had a weird tingling sensation in your mouth? Chances are that your pineapple was not yet ripe. A ripe pineapple will be firm to the touch, but will also give way slightly when pushed. If the outside feels soft and even a bit mushy, it is overripe. Smelling the pineapple is another way to gauge ripeness. If it smells sweet, then it is most likely ripe and ready to eat; if it is odourless, then it's not ready. A ripe pineapple will also exhibit a beautiful golden yellow colour starting from the bottom and moving upward. If the pineapple is completely green, it is not yet ripe.

**1 ripe pineapple, sliced into chunks
1/3 cup (75 mL) chocolate (or caramel) syrup
1 Tbsp (15 mL) shredded coconut**

Prepare campfire, or preheat grill to low. Soak wooden skewers in water for 30 minutes (or use metal skewers).

Thread pineapple pieces onto skewers and heat for about 2 minutes per side. Remove pineapple from skewers and place on plate. Drizzle chocolate sauce over warm pineapple and sprinkle with coconut.

Dutch Oven Cobbler

Serves 8

I must admit that I am not a huge fan of desserts; however, this Dutch Oven Cobbler is simply to die for. And without any thick pie crust, it is fairly low in fat. I am a huge supporter of the Dutch oven for outdoor recipes, so I decided to give this one a try. Because this cobbler requires at least 1 hour of cooking time, I knew my fire needed to be a good one, so I planned accordingly. The coals required to sear a steak are much different than the coals required for most Dutch oven dishes. The real trick is in the timing. You do not want to start this meal too early before your fire is ready, or leave it too late so that your coals peter out. I am proud to say that my first attempt at Dutch Oven Cobbler was received with rave reviews!

1 × 15 oz (425 mL) can fruit cocktail, with juice
1 × 15 oz (425 mL) can sliced peaches, with juice
1 × 12 oz (341 mL) can pineapple chunks, with juice
1/2 tsp (2 mL) ground cinnamon
1 × 8 1/4 oz (517 g) box golden (or yellow) cake mix, dry
1 cup (250 mL) brown sugar
1/2 cup (125 mL) butter, cut into pieces

Prepare campfire (*see* Tip). In Dutch oven, combine fruit cocktail, peaches, pineapple, all fruit juices and cinnamon, and stir well. Sprinkle dry golden cake mix over top and sprinkle brown sugar on top of cake mix. Place little pieces of butter of top of brown sugar. Cook, covered, over coals for about 1 hour until top is browned and cake has absorbed fruit juices.

 COOKING ON COALS

You will need to start off with a good-sized campfire in order to produce enough coals to sustain at least 1 hour of cooking time.

Fruit Bannock

Serves 6

Bannock is about as traditional a Canadian food as any I can think of. It is believed to have been brought to Canada by European settlers. The early voyageurs and trappers brought this Scottish bread dish to native communities across Canada, where it soon was adopted as a staple of many of those First Nations. Bannock can be baked on an open fire using a stick, a pan or even a hot rock. Today, this traditional bread has been spruced up and is served with a variety of different ingredients, including fruit, nuts, meat and fish.

3 cups (750 mL) flour
1 tsp (5 mL) salt
2 Tbsp (30 mL) baking powder
1/2 cup (125 mL) diced apple, or blueberries
1/4 cup (60 mL) shortening, melted
1 1/2 cups (375 mL) water
2 Tbsp (30 mL) sugar

Prepare campfire, or preheat grill to medium. In large bowl, combine flour, salt, baking powder and fruit. Make well in centre and add shortening and water. Stir to form ball. Place ball on work surface and knead gently for 10 minutes.

Pat dough into circle about 1 inch (2.5 cm) thick. Cook in greased frying pan for 15 minutes on each side. Sprinkle with sugar and serve hot.

Sweets and Drinks

Wilderness Chocolate Fondue

Serves 4

No matter what style of camping trip I go on, I always bring a plastic storage bin I call my tickle trunk. Inside is a collection of crucial items: 3 flashlights (1 LED, 1 crank-style, 1 disposable), fire igniters, foil, several candles, a bottle of vegetable oil, camphor blocks (for the outhouse), paper towel, a Zippo lighter with extra lighter fluid, fire starter sticks, a Fox 40 whistle (for safety), a can of bear spray, cast-iron pans, cooking pots, a coffee percolator, an extra can of naphtha gas, a small hatchet, a filleting knife, sugar, flour, salt, pepper, a picnic table cover (with clips), a camp toast maker, a handheld GPS unit, two-way radios with fresh batteries, and finally a transistor radio. Yes, it may seem a little over the top, but being prepared when spending time outdoors can make all the difference.

1 1/2 cups (375 mL) chocolate chips (fondue chocolate)
1 cup (250 mL) cream (18%)
sliced strawberries, bananas and apples
pineapple chunks
white or red grapes

Prepare campfire, or preheat grill to low. In small pot, heat chocolate chips and cream until chocolate is melted and slightly bubbling. Remove from heat and either transfer to fondue pot or serve from pot. Use fondue forks to dip fruit into chocolate mixture. Yummy.

Chocolate Cherry Coffee

Serves 2

The only thing better than sitting by the fire late at night warming yourself up with your favourite homemade hot beverage is enjoying it first thing in the morning. You will find the added sweetness of this over-the-open-fire Chocolate Cherry Coffee to be the cat's meow while camping. I always keep a few candy bars handy when spending time outdoors—you never know when you might need them.

> 2 cups (500 mL) cold water
> 2 Tbsp (30 mL) coffee grounds
> 1 milk chocolate bar
> 4 to 6 seedless black cherries

Prepare campfire. In saucepan, bring water to a boil. Add coffee grounds directly to boiling water. Stir while water boils until coffee is desired strength. Remove from heat and add chocolate bar. Stir until chocolate has melted. Using a spoon to hold back coffee grounds, pour into 2 coffee mugs. Place cherries in mugs.

Homemade Hot Cocoa

Serves 1

My daughters Emily and Grace are two of the biggest hot cocoa fans I know, and over the years they have acquired a taste for the real thing—plain old chocolate syrup and milk just doesn't cut it anymore. This Homemade Hot Cocoa recipe dates back to when I was a boy in the 1970s and Mom would prepare a steaming cup of "the good stuff" for me after a long day of playing outdoors. I am proud to carry on the tradition with my own children nearly 40 years later.

> 1 cup (250 mL) milk
> 1 Tbsp (15 mL) cocoa
> 1 Tbsp (15 mL) sugar
> pinch of salt
> marshmallows

Prepare campfire. In small saucepan, combine milk, cocoa, sugar and salt and mix well. Heat, stirring constantly, until cocoa starts to boil gently. Continue to boil gently for 2 minutes. Remove and serve with marshmallows on top.

Recipe Index

171

172

175

About the Author

Growing up in a family-owned hotel in the Laurentian Mountains of rural Québec, Jeff was introduced to the outdoors and great cooking at a very young age, falling in love with both instantly. Over the years, he has made the great outdoors a focal point for his life's work. Jeff has a degree in environmental management as well as fish and wildlife biology. He is an award-winning member of the Outdoor Writers of Canada and has contributed to several Canadian and American publications over the years. He currently writes for Newfoundland's popular *Outdoor Sportsman* magazine and *Outdoor Canada* magazine, and has a regular column in *Bounder Magazine*. His first book, *Weird Facts about Fishing*, was released in 2010, and he writes a popular blog, *The Outdoors Guy*, for the *Ottawa Sun*.

Jeff has travelled to each and every province from coast to coast—hunting, fishing, camping and enjoying the fruits of his labour. He describes himself as the consummate conservationist and family-man, and describes his cooking as down to earth, simple, and about as Canadian as you can get. Jeff spent a lot of time at his uncle's famous steakhouse in the mountains of Québec, and picked up copious down-home tips along the way. He brings with him an in-depth knowledge of nature and conservation and a genuine love and passion for the outdoors—from the field to the table.